EXPOSITORY STUDIES IN GENESIS 4-11

EXPOSITORY STUDIES IN GENESIS 4-11

THE BEGINNINGS

RAY C. STEDMAN

WORD BOOKS
PUBLISHER
4800 WEST WACO DRIVE
WACO, TEXAS
76703

EXPOSITORY STUDIES IN GENESIS 4-11: *The Beginnings*

Copyright © 1978 by Ray C. Stedman. All rights reserved. No part of this book may be reproduced in any form, except for brief quotations in reviews, without written permission of the publisher.

Quotations from the Revised Standard Version of the Bible, copyright 1946 (renewed 1973), 1956 and © 1971 by the Division of Christian Education of the National Council of the Churches of Christ in the USA, and are used by permission.

Discovery Books are published by Word Books, Publisher in cooperation with Discovery Foundation, Palo Alto, California.

Library of Congress catalog card number: 77-83286

Printed in the United States of America

ISBN 0-8499-2818-4

First Printing, January 1978
Second Printing, July 1978
Third Printing, September 1981

Contents

Preface

In a companion series of studies from Genesis called *Understanding Man,* I focussed on the true nature of man as revealed in that section of the Scriptures (Gen. 2:4—3:24). Of course that was not an exhaustive study of man; the whole Bible is in part an elaboration of this fascinating subject. Furthermore, as we look at the famous characters in the chapters comprising the current study—Cain and Abel, Enoch, Noah, Nimrod, and a doomed cast of thousands—we certainly have some additional pointed insights into the nature of man.

But in these chapters (Gen. 4—11:26) relating early human history we also see the underlying threads of all human society, for all time. Moses has provided us with a very sturdy framework for understanding ourselves—in society—which is how most of us live, give or take a few hermits.

The general and persistent thrust of mankind is to band together, even though the result is nearly always disastrous. In one place we can see bumper stickers proclaiming that "We Are One," while in another place there are signs announcing the rules of apartheid. There are tides, upheavals, and movements in human society which no sociologist can come to grips with apart from understanding the reasons for them as given to us in the Bible.

These reasons are not spelled out as such. They are presented as parables and left for us to understand, if we will. Without doubt, there was a real Cain, there was a genuine 40-day deluge, there was a solid gopher-wood ark, and there was an actual tower of babbling confusion. There is no need to question the historicity of these events, nor is it my intent to prove them historical. I believe they are, but further, that they are recorded so as to teach us graphically the principles upon which man has built his society, and the inherent flaws in those principles. The point is not simply to accuse man; God's point, always, is to show a better way.

Part of the process of discovering God's way is first to come to an understanding of the dismal effects of man's way. Always the bad news precedes the good news. The cross precedes the resurrection. But keep in mind that the expulsion from Eden was also the beginning of redemption, the first step into the kingdom of God.

We are all more than individuals; we are political beings. We struggle to understand how to live in community —especially, in recent years, in the Christian community. But we will fail, with the best of intentions, unless we understand what Moses has set before us in the chronicle of the beginnings of man in his first attempts to live in society.

EXPOSITORY STUDIES IN GENESIS 4-11

1

The Devil's Opportunity

HISTORY, AS WE KNOW IT, is largely the story of the wars, battles, and bloodshed of mankind. It is the chronicle of man's progress from the primitive ax to machine guns, napalm, and nuclear explosions. But why is this? Why has humanity throughout the entire space of its history wrestled unendingly with this terrible problem of human hatred and bloodshed? The shallow answers which have been given, such as economics, adventure, greed, power politics, have all long since been shown to be insufficient and superficial, though you still hear them echoed from time to time. The key to our twentieth-century dilemma actually lies in a story that took place at the dawn of history, the story of two brothers. The account begins in chapter 4 of Genesis:

Now Adam knew Eve his wife, and she conceived and bore Cain, saying, "I have gotten a man with the help of the Lord." And again, she bore his brother Abel. Now Abel was a keeper of sheep, and Cain a tiller of the ground. In the course of time Cain brought to the Lord an offering of the fruit of the ground, and Abel brought of the firstlings of his flock and of their fat portions. And the Lord had regard for Abel and his offering, but for Cain and his offering he had no regard. So Cain was very angry, and his countenance fell. The Lord said to Cain, "Why are you angry, and why has your countenance fallen? If you do well, will you not be accepted? And if you do not do well, sin is crouching at the door; its desire is for you, but you must master it." Cain said to Abel his brother, "Let us go out to the field." And when they were in the field, Cain rose up against his brother Abel, and killed him (Gen. 4:1–8).

Here we have what is obviously a highly condensed account. This story undoubtedly covers a span of many years—perhaps more than thirty or forty years, or even as many as a hundred. We are not told how old the two were when Cain slew Abel, but undoubtedly they had grown into manhood and most likely were in their early thirties. The story begins with the birth of Cain and the joy of his mother, Eve, and it centers on three highly important matters: the naming of the boys; the offerings which each presented; and the reaction of Cain to God's rejection of his offering.

Let us begin with this name, Cain. It is a very significant name because, as the account tells us, it means "gotten" and comes from the Hebrew word, *ganah*, which means, "to get." You will recognize it is as the derivation for our English word, "begotten." We speak of begetting our children, and this comes from the name, Cain. The text says Eve named him Cain because, as she said, "I have gotten a man with the help of the Lord."

That latter phrase is a bit weak in translation. It is not merely "with the help of the Lord" (which is true of every birth), but what Eve probably said was, "I have gotten a man, *even the Lord.*" By that she was referring to the great promise God had given her, saying she would bring forth a seed who would bruise the serpent's head (Gen. 3:15). She understood that the "seed" would be a divine Being, so when her first child was born—a male— she felt perfectly justified in naming him, "Gotten." "I have gotten a man, even the Lord."

It is characteristic of predictions in the Bible that they do not often include a time element. Eve apparently had no idea how long it would be before this promise would be fulfilled. Remember that Jesus said to his disciples, "It is not for you to know times or seasons which the Father has fixed by his own authority" (Acts 1:7). We can never know precisely when great predicted events are going to be fulfilled, though we can often know when they are approaching fulfillment, as in the case of the second coming of the Lord.

Seeds of Arrogance

Now when the second child is born an ominous element enters the story, for the name of this child is Abel, which means "frail." This suggests that already the physical effects of sin were becoming apparent in the race. The second child born into history was perhaps a frail, sickly child, so he was given the name, Abel. But regardless of whether or not this was physically true, this name certainly suggests that there was a difference in the attitude of the parents toward the children. Adam and Eve regarded these boys in two different ways: Cain was the strong one; Abel the weaker. It would be very natural for them to favor Cain as the firstborn, the stronger of the two, born "under a lucky star," a child of destiny, one designed perhaps to fulfill great promise. Perhaps this strong hint of favoritism right at the beginning offers an explanation for what follows in the story. Already, at the very birth of these two boys, the seeds of arrogance and conceit have been planted in the heart of Cain by his unsuspecting parents simply by the way they treat their children. How significant that is—and how frightening! Sometimes seeds can be planted in early childhood that will come to fruit many years later, bringing heartache and despair to parents. (The interesting thing here is that it is not the neglected child who suffers most, but the favored one. I will leave that for all amateur psychologists to chew on.)

Now the scene shifts to a much later time. The boys are grown and are supporting themselves. Cain is a rugged farmer, a tiller of the soil. But that work is obviously too hard for Abel, and he becomes a keeper of the sheep. This indicates that from the earliest dawn of history mankind has understood and been involved in agricultural and pastoral pursuits. He was not, as we sometimes gather from dioramas in our museums, originally a hunter only.

A Time and a Place

We are now told that in the course of time both Cain and Abel brought an offering to God. There are two things strongly implied by this account. First, it is clear that there was a prescribed time indicated for the bringing of an offering. The phrase which in our version is translated, "In the course of time," is, in the Hebrew, "At the end of days." This is a strong suggestion that there was a definitely prescribed period. Perhaps it was once a year, at the end of days—i.e., at the end of the winter season, just before spring.

Second, it is clear from this account that a prescribed place existed for this offering. They were to bring it "before the Lord," to a definite place. There they were to appear in the presence of the Lord. If you link this with the closing words of chapter 3, there is a clear suggestion that when God set the cherubim and flaming sword at the gateway to Eden, he thereby created a mercy seat. Many centuries later, when the divine pattern was given to Moses for making the tabernacle, it included a mercy seat with cherubim, whose wings would meet over the mercy seat. That was the place where offerings were to be placed. The Day of Atonement was consummated at the mercy seat when once a year the High Priest brought in a lamb for all the people. Perhaps this traces from this earliest account of an offering. Thus, it is very likely that at the gateway of Eden was a mercy seat, where once a year Adam and Eve and their children were to come with an offering for the Lord.

In passing, I want you to note that Adam and Eve had evidently taught their boys all that they knew and had learned of God, and had trained them to worship. Man, in his primitive condition, was not groping blindly after God, seeking through centuries of patient endeavor to find his way to an understanding of divine truth. Mankind began on that level, as Paul makes clear in Romans: Men who knew God, who knew who he was, departed from that knowledge and turned to idolatry. The sons of Adam and Eve knew everything their parents knew about God.

When we come to the offerings Cain and Abel bring to God, however, we see a significant difference between the two men. Cain's offering of fruit was instantly rejected, but Abel's lamb was accepted. How that rejection and acceptance were indicated we are not told, though perhaps we might find a clue from the stories of Gideon and, later on, of Elijah on Mount Carmel. When these men offered to God, fire came down from heaven and consumed their offerings. This was the indication of its acceptance by God. We can, of course, make much of the fact that Cain ought to have known better than to bring an offering of fruit to God. He surely knew from his father that God had cursed the ground, and to offer the fruit of a cursed ground to God was obviously to insult him. Also I think we can say that Adam and Eve and Cain and Abel unquestionably knew the most basic truth which the Word of God labors to get across to us, and which runs through the entire length of Scripture. It is given to us in Hebrews: "Without the shedding of blood there is no forgiveness of sins" (Heb. 9:22).

Why is that so important? Primarily because it is designed to teach us something crucial. All these symbols of the Old Testament are designed to teach us important things, so what is it that this teaches us—"Without the shedding of blood there is no forgiveness of sins."? It teaches that the problem of sin is no light matter. It cannot be handled by a good resolution or an earnest resolve. It is not settled by simply deciding to turn over a new leaf, or to change one's attitude. Sin is something that is embedded in the race and touches the springs of life. It can only be solved by death. That, of course, is what ultimately explains the cross of Jesus Christ. In his coming, he could not merely teach us good things; in order to deal with the problem of sin, he had to die.

A Smile to a Frown

But I do not want to dwell on this now. Although I think it is clearly here, it is not the heart of this story.

The account says that Cain was angry at God's rejection of his offering and his countenance fell. Obviously, he came expecting God to accept his offering. Perhaps he was very pleased with himself. Perhaps he felt that his offering of fruit and grain was much more beautiful, much more aesthetically pleasant than the bloody, dirty thing that Abel put on the altar. But when the smoke rose from Abel's offering and his own remained untouched, Cain's smile changed to a frown. He was angry and resentful, and the whole appearance of his face altered.

How well we know this feeling! And for the same reason—jealousy! Cain was jealous because his brother was accepted and he was rejected. As the New Testament tells us, he was angry "because his own deeds were evil and his brother's righteous" (1 Jn. 3:12). Is it not amazing the things that make us jealous? We are jealous because our neighbor has a bigger car than we have, or his child plays with a doll that can talk, while our children have to play with some cheap little thing from the 5 & 10¢ store. . . . Our fellow worker has a desk that is nearer to the window than ours. . . . Or perhaps he gets a longer notice of commendation in the company paper than we do, or he has softer carpets on the floor, or he has two windows instead of one in his office. It is amazing how such petty matters can cause us to rankle with feelings of envy and resentment.

The basic reason underlying our resentment is the very reason Cain was angry. He did not like the way God was acting. He did not like what God had chosen to do for Abel. With him it was not a question of being upset, theologically, because fruit was not as good as a lamb. There is no implication of that in this story. From our perspective we can see such implications, but that was not what was troubling Cain. What bothered him was simply that God did not conform to his idea of rightness. When God presumes to cut across the grain of our expectations, we are all offended, aren't we? We are quick with the question, How can God do a thing like this? Why does God permit this? It is all because we want *our* thoughts to be the program on which God operates. When he presumes to do anything else, we get angry with him. Oh, it is true that in a church service we can all nod our heads at Isaiah's words, "God's thoughts are not our thoughts nor his ways our ways." But when he actually begins to act on that basis, how upset it makes us! We feel that he has betrayed us, played us false in some way.

A Simple Question

But notice God's grace. He does not flare back at Cain with thunderbolts of judgment. He simply asks him a question, "Why are you angry, and why has your countenance fallen?" That is the best question to ask a jealous, resentful individual. Why? Think it through, now; why are you so angry? Why are you filled with resentment against this person? I have learned that when men and women ask me, as they sometimes do: Why does this have to happen to me? What have I done that I should have to go through this thing? The only proper answer is: Why shouldn't you? These things happen to everyone and to anyone; why shouldn't it happen to you? Why should you escape? Why should you resent it? Why should you assume that you have special privilege or an immunity to the normal problems, injustices, and trials of life?

That is a hard question to answer, isn't it? But notice that God goes on to light a lamp of warning before Cain. He says, "If you do well, will you not be accepted?" What does he mean here by "doing well"? He is certainly not saying, "Well, Cain, just do your best. Try hard to please me and everything will be all right." It has a specific meaning here. It means, "If you bring the acceptable offering; if you will go to your brother and trade some of your grain for one of his lambs and bring that lamb, whose blood is to be shed for the remission of sins, indicating that you understand at least something of the problem that sin proposes, then you too will be accepted. It is not too late. I'm not going to judge you now. You can go back and repent, you can change, and if you do well in this way, you will be accepted just like Abel, for I am no respecter of persons. It is truth that I deal with," says God, "and I don't care what kind of a past a person has; I will accept anyone who determines to act in truth and honesty."

But if not, then look out! Beware! If you let this moment pass, says God to Cain, watch out! Now that it has all been made clear to you, if you refuse to repent, to go back and bring the right offering, watch out. Sin is crouching at the door of your life like a lion, ready to jump on you, to seize you, and to destroy you. God is saying to Cain and to us: Don't treat jealousy or resentment lightly, because it is not a light thing. If you let it fester, you will soon find yourself in the grip of a power greater than you can handle, and you will do things that you didn't ever think you would do.

Have you found that out? I certainly have. Whenever we let resentment against God fester in our heart, and then stuff it all down inside and fondle it and play with it, sooner or later we will say something we didn't intend to say or do something that we didn't intend to do.

This is what happened here. Cain disregards God's warning, refuses to repent—nursing his jealousy along—and soon his mind conceives a diabolical plot, a way to get even. How powerfully it makes its appeal to him. Ah-hah, he thinks, now I've got him. That brother of mine who thinks he's so good, who thinks he's so holy, now I've got him! With a disarming smile he comes to Abel and says, "Brother, let's go out into the fields and talk." And there the murderous ax rises and falls and Abel sinks to the ground with a smashed skull, murdered by his brother's hand.

Murder by Insult

What makes a man kill his brother? During the Vietnam war I remember seeing a picture in a news magazine of a Vietnamese officer executing a captured Viet Cong. When that picture appeared, someone wrote a letter to the editor commenting on it. The letter said, "What a terrible thing! There stands that turtle-headed little man pointing a pistol at this man's head and shooting him in cold blood. How can a man do a thing like that!" In the next issue a very provocative and perceptive reply appeared: "The reader asks, 'What causes a man to act like that?' The answer is: the same thing that causes someone to call another person 'a turtle-headed little man!' "

It is true, isn't it? It *is* the same thing. Have you noticed how often Scripture links insult and murder together? For example, there are those scorching words from the lips of Jesus, in the Sermon on the Mount:

> "You have heard that it was said to the men of old, 'You shall not kill; and whoever kills shall be liable to judgment.' But I say to you that every one who is angry with his brother shall be liable to judgment; whoever insults his brother shall be liable to the council, and whoever says, 'You fool!' shall be liable to the hell of fire. So if you are offering your gift at the altar, and there remem-

ber that your brother has something against you, leave your gift there before the altar and go; first be reconciled to your brother, and then come and offer your gift" (Matt. 5:21–24).

John tells us that if we hate our brother, we have murdered him in God's sight. What he is really telling us is that we refrain from killing the ones we resent only because we fear reprisal. It was a very frequent occurrence in the days of the Old West for someone to simply draw a gun and shoot a person out of a momentary irritation. Why? Because there was no law to take reprisal against him. He could immediately express what he felt in his heart.

Do you see how far removed our thoughts are from those of God? What we regard as trivialities, mere peccadillos or trifles, he sees as monstrous, terrible things threatening our peace, our health, and life itself. So he tries to warn Cain: "Cain, you don't know what you are doing. If you let this thing rankle in your heart, before you know it you will have killed your brother." In the letter to the Ephesians the apostle Paul says, "Do not let the sun go down on your anger, and [thus] give no opportunity to the devil" (Eph. 4:26–27). There the devil is, waiting like a roaring lion, crouching at the door, ready to spring on you if you give him an opportunity. What is the opportunity? Allowing your wrath to last beyond the setting of the sun, to carry it over into another day, to form a grudge, a permanent dislike for an individual. When you do that, the door is wide open and nothing can stop Satan from beginning to poison your life and destroy you.

The New Testament tells us to be at peace with one another. We are not even to let our worship delay us in making peace. If you bring your gift and there remem-

ber that your brother has something against you—or you
have something against him—leave your gift and go to
your brother. Be reconciled, then come and settle things
with God. That judges me! Does it not judge you? In the
light of this story, how much we can see that the evil of
our day springs out of these seeds of dislike for one another and of refusal to repent when the grace of God
warns us of the power we are dealing with.

How about you? Are you angry with someone? Do you
harbor a grudge in your heart? Are you holding resentment against another individual? Are you seething with
hurt feelings because of something someone has said—
perhaps years ago—or even weeks ago? What about it?
If you do well, if you bring the offering that God has provided, if you offer the forgiveness which he makes possible, you will be accepted. Peace will flow again into your
heart and life, and with it, health and strength. But if
you allow it to fester, to lie there unsettled, it will master
you.

*Our Father, you who know our hearts, deal earnestly
among us that we will not lightly put these things aside.
Help us, Lord, to realize that the wolves are now howl-
ing in the cellars of our nation's soul because of the unjudged dislikes of Christians toward one another, the
unsettled resentments that have grown into family feuds
that have gone on for weeks and months and years. God
grant to us grace to deal with this matter in the way that
has been so abundantly provided by the sacrifice of the
Lord Jesus on our behalf, so that we may be tender-
hearted, forgiving one another, even as God for Christ's
sake has forgiven us. We pray in his name. Amen.*

2

The Mark of Cain

WE HAVE NOW EXAMINED the causes for human hatred and warfare and have seen that wars and murders spring from seeds of unreasoning jealousy and envy which are allowed to lie unjudged in human hearts. Men kill because they hate; they hate because they will not accept God's ordering of life. They want their own way, they want God to act as they want him to act (or perhaps I should say, as *we* want him to act).

Now we come to a very closely related problem which has at various times threatened to tear our nation apart: the problem of race relations, of human brotherhood:

> Then the Lord said to Cain, "Where is Abel your brother?" He said, "I do not know; am I my brother's keeper?" (Gen. 4:9).

25

Cain's insolent and arrogant response to God's question is a sign of his inward unacknowledged guilt. This is always the way of guilt—to disclaim responsibility. Cain replies, "My brother? What have I to do with my brother? Am I my brother's keeper? Is it my responsibility to know where my brother is?" The hypocrisy of that is most evident. Though Cain could disclaim responsibility for knowing where his brother was, he did not hesitate to assume the far greater responsibility of taking his brother's life.

We hear much of the same thing today. In 1968 we were reeling from the shock of the murder of Dr. Martin Luther King. Many in those days were saying things like this: "Well, it's not our fault that Dr. King was killed. Why should we suffer for what some fanatic did? It's not our responsibility." Others said, "He ought to have known this would happen. After all, if you stir up trouble, sooner or later you will pay the price for it." No one can deny the logic and truth of a statement like that. Yet it is very obviously incomplete, and there is nothing in it of facing responsibility and no honest answering of the terrible question from Cain's lips, "Am I my brother's keeper?"

I believe we were all guilty of the death of Dr. Martin Luther King, Jr. and for all that precipitated and made that death inevitable. We are guilty now, every one of us who has permitted the unspoken dictates of our society to keep us from forming friendships with black people, or who has refused to break through the barriers which have silently and powerfully been raised by prejudice, pride, and isolation.

The rioting over civil rights has in large measure died down now. And yet the issue is still unsolved, or unresolved. Most of us are content to breathe a sigh of relief and return to our comforts, without having been touched by what happened in those turbulent days.

Two or three decades ago Dr. Carl Henry wrote a book called "The Uneasy Conscience of Fundamentalism," which bothered many people when it first came out. In it Dr. Henry pointed out that the isolationism which many Christians adopt, the isolationism which removes us from contact with non-Christians, has also successfully removed us from grappling with some of the pressing social questions of our hour. We have often been quite content to sing about going to heaven, but have shown very little concern for the sick and the poor, the lonely, the old, and the miserable of our world. Isaiah 58 is a ringing condemnation of such an attitude on the part of religious people. Other passages from the Scriptures make clear that God is infinitely concerned in this area of life, and those who bear his name dare not neglect these areas. Let us be perfectly frank and honest and admit that this is a manifestation of Christian love which we evangelicals have tended greatly to neglect. The evangelical church, therefore, has largely become almost exclusively white, middle-class, Protestant, and Republican.

I have nothing against any of those designations except that their preponderance indicates something is wrong with the church. The church was never intended to minister only to one segment of society, but is to include all people, all classes, all colors, without distinction. Both the Old and New Testament are crystal clear in this respect. These distinctions are to be ignored in the church. They must be, otherwise we are not being faithful to the One who called us and who, himself, was the Friend of sinners—of all kinds.

Because this neglect is rather obvious, even though we sometimes shut our eyes to it, it has precipitated a violent rejection of Christianity by many. I ran across this poem once which expresses very forcefully what many are thinking, especially among the young people, about the church:

> Fat, old, smug church.
> What are you waiting for?
> Where is your Christ? Up in the sky?
> Back in the past? Somewhere else?
> There's a painted whore down at the bar.
> Do you care?
> There's a Negro family that can't find a home.
> Do you care?
> There's a hippy, high on LSD
> Who in hell cares?
> Who in heaven cares?
> You fat, old, useless church!

That picture is overdrawn, granted, but it is true enough to hurt. We must be perfectly honest and admit that this has been the weak spot of evangelical life—this failure to move out in obedience to God's command to offer love, friendship, forgiveness, and grace to all people without regard to class, color, background, or heredity. We believe that the gospel is salt for preserving society from corruption, and that in calling out "the mystery of godliness," God is forming a secret society which constitutes the church as a counteraction to "the mystery of lawlessness" which is also at work. These are opposed, one to the other, and when lawlessness surges to the front as it has today and seems to flow unchecked through the cities of our nation, it is because the mystery of godliness has been thwarted and held back, contained, and not turned loose in the midst of society.

If we still are reluctant to face some of the things this passage brings before us, perhaps we need to look on to Cain's punishment, given in verses 10 through 12.

And the Lord said, "What have you done? The voice of your brother's blood is crying to me from the ground. And now you are cursed from the ground, which has opened its mouth to receive your brother's blood from your hand. When you till the ground, it shall no longer yield to you its strength; you shall be a fugitive and a wanderer on the earth" (Gen. 4:10–12).

God uses a very vivid figure here to describe his knowledge of Cain's deed. Cain thought he was acting in secret, but of course everything is open before God. God said, "The blood of your brother is crying to me, shrieking to me, from the ground." Abel's blood shouts to God. It makes demands upon his justice and his love. Hebrews refers to the blood of Jesus, which speaks "more graciously than the blood of Abel" (Heb. 12:24). We know what that means. The blood of Jesus is crying out before God for forgiveness: "Father, forgive them, for they know not what they do." The blood of Jesus is crying constantly for mercy, for grace to all who take refuge under it, and thus it does speak more graciously than the blood of Abel.

But the blood of Abel speaks, too. That is what God is saying to Cain. "Your brother's blood is crying something out to me that I can't ignore. It is shrieking to me from the ground." Crying for what? For redress, for vengeance, for justice, for the righting of wrong. It cries to a God of justice and says, "Do not let this deed go unavenged. Do something about this." Now notice carefully that it is crying out for vengeance from God, not man. "Vengeance belongs to me," says the Lord. It never belongs to man. In fact, when man assumes that role, he only makes things worse. He unleashes a vicious cycle which escalates rapidly into all-out anarchy, sometimes civil war, and revolution. But nevertheless, God is driven to act. That is what this ancient story of Cain and Abel tells us. God cannot allow these things to occur without responding. His sense of justice must do something about the murderous act.

What then does God do? He sentences Cain! He assigns a punishment to him, and the nature of it is very significant. Notice, there are no thunderbolts of wrath here. God does not seize hold of Cain and take his life in vengeance. What happens is what writers sometimes call "poetic justice," i.e., a strangely fitting result. Cain was a man of the soil, a tiller of the ground, and in this work he took pride and found joy. A man's work is always his pride. Cain was a farmer who delighted in producing beautiful crops of fruit and grain. But now he has poured the blood of his brother upon the ground. So now the ground, the arena of his pride, will be cursed. It will no longer yield him its strength. He will find, in his attempts to work the ground, nothing but frustration, sweat, tears, and toil.

Cain, in other words, has lost his "green thumb." The ground will no longer release its fruitfulness to him; his working of the ground will be fruitless labor. He will therefore be forced to wander from place to place, as the crops fail wherever he goes. He will find himself unable to make a living anywhere, so he will become a wanderer on the face of the earth.

I wonder if we are not still hearing echoes of this strange sentence upon Cain today. What is the pride of America? In what have we most taken pride? Is it not in our great American cities—these great showplaces of wealth and power—these planned communities which we intended to be models of knowledge, wisdom, and happiness, where all the problems of life would be happily solved?

But what has happened? Because we would not answer

God's question, "Where is your brother?" and we replied, as Cain, in arrogance and defiance, "Am I my brother's keeper?" from time to time smoke rises from American cities. The streets of our cities are filled with broken glass, stores are looted, riots threaten, and homes are burned. The pride and glory of America is severely threatened at this very hour, and we have not seen the worst of it yet. But to me, the ultimate fate is not the physical violence which threatens our nation, but the fact that America has lost its way home. American families no longer know how to have a home. We have become wanderers—lonely, empty, restless; a nation on wheels, driven, and homeless —vainly seeking to find something to satisfy. We are fugitives from a pitiless fate.

But the account closes on a hopeful note:

> Cain said to the Lord, "My punishment is greater than I can bear. Behold, thou hast driven me this day away from the ground; and from thy face I shall be hidden; and I shall be a fugitive and a wanderer on the earth, and whoever finds me will slay me." Then the Lord said to him, "Not so! If any one slays Cain, vengeance shall be taken on him sevenfold." And the Lord put a mark on Cain, lest any who came upon him should kill him. Then Cain went away from the presence of the Lord, and dwelt in the land of Nod [which means "the land of wandering"], east of Eden (Gen. 4:13–16).

It is obvious from this account that Cain fears the vengeance of his other brothers. You ask, "What other brothers?" In the very next chapter, verse 4, we are told plainly that Adam and Eve "had other sons and daughters" besides the ones named in the Scripture. This is the answer to the question many have asked out of a kind of naive ignorance, "Where did Cain get his wife?" The answer is, he married one of his sisters. This was still a common occurrence as late as the days of Abraham, who married his half-sister. But Cain knows that his life is in danger wherever he goes. Wherever he is, he will run into relatives (can you imagine anything worse?) who will be motivated either by fear or vengeance to take his life.

Cain now is obsessed with his guilt, haunted by it. He knows he can go nowhere in human society without constantly wondering if people's attitudes toward him are sinister ones, or whether they are friendly and can be trusted. Out of his obsession with guilt he says to God, "My punishment is greater than I can bear. I will live in constant danger of reprisal." But God says, "No, you won't." And God puts a mark upon him (which has now become a proverb) by which, as he says, "Any one who sees this mark will know that God himself protects Cain, and whoever takes this life will be avenged sevenfold."

I do not know what the mark of Cain was. It is impossible to tell whether it was some physical mark, some sign in his body which indicated that he was God's property, or something else. Perhaps it was a hopeless, pathetic look that would stir pity in people's hearts, so that Cain became an object of universal pity to those who saw him. The point is that even the guilty man is still God's property! God throws a circle of protective love about Cain and says, "Yes, he is guilty. He's a murderer—but he is still my property, and don't forget it in your dealings with him."

Mark of Grace

The mark of Cain, then, is not a mark of shame, as we usually interpret it. It is not a mark to brand him in the eyes of others as a terrible murderer to be shunned and treated as a pariah. It is, rather, a mark of grace by which God is saying, "This man is still my property. Hands off!" The heart of God is always ready to show mercy. There can only be one reason why God thus protected Cain. It was in order to give him time to think and to repent. This is ever the way of God. In 2 Peter we are admonished not to make the mistake of regarding the longsuffering of God as weakness. There are those who seem to feel that since twenty centuries of Christian life have gone by and nothing has happened that God will never do anything to right wrongs. Don't make the mistake of thinking that God is impotent. Rather, Peter says that it is his mercy; it is his grace, giving men time to repent in order that none may perish but that all may come to repentance (2 Pet. 3:9). Thus God gives even Cain a moment of grace, space to repent.

Is this not what God is saying to America in this hour? The time is short. We must not treat these events lightly that are happening in our country today. These are not isolated instances; they are not merely something that will all blow over, as trouble has sometimes blown over in the past. Violent incidents represent outbreaks of long-suppressed abuse that finally breaks through. It can no longer be contained, nor can we dismiss it with a wave of the hand. We hold the key to correction and relief. When God said to Nineveh, "Yet forty days shall this city be overthrown," from the king down to the commonest person they repented in sackcloth and ashes, in genuineness of contrition for their evil acts. Even though Jonah's nose was put out of joint because God showed mercy, God nevertheless withheld his judging hand from the city, and it was not until a hundred years later that Nineveh was destroyed, as God had predicted. So we must take a saving message to the oppressed and disadvantaged in our society.

Recently, a number of us had the privilege of meeting

in fellowship with Dr. Edward Hill, a black pastor from the Watts area in Los Angeles—a wonderful, gifted, gracious man of God. He told us that only the day before Dr. Martin Luther King, Jr., was murdered he had said to some white friends, "If you white people ever pray for any colored man, then pray for Dr. Martin Luther King. He is the one who is doing more to restrain the forces of radicalism and violence among the Negroes than any other person, and you ought to be holding him up in prayer." Then he told of his own experience.

"Seventeen years ago," he said, "my heart was as filled with hatred and bitterness against white people as any black Muslim today." Raised in Houston, Edward Hill was exposed to the usual treatment of blacks in the South: white and colored waiting rooms, white and colored drinking fountains, white and colored seats on buses and trains, etc. All of these created in him a boiling bitterness and hatred against whites. But one day he joined a singing group led by a white man, a pastor. When they went out on their first trip together, the leader of the group called them together and said something that struck home to Ed Hill's heart and was the opening wedge for the gospel of grace: "Now look, we're going out into various places to sing together, and we're going to be pilgrims in a strange country. We are like strangers going out to a different land. In some places some of our members are going to be asked to eat in the kitchen. When they are asked to eat in the kitchen, we're all going to eat in the kitchen. When some are asked to use a certain restroom, we'll all use that restroom because we're pilgrims together."

Dr. Hill said, "I couldn't believe my ears. At first I thought it was a joke and that he was just putting on a show. But as I traveled with that man, I saw that he meant what he said. For the first time I understood the love of

Jesus Christ, and that finally led me to accept him." Thus a man who gladly assumed the role of his brother's keeper found a way to a bitter young man's heart and kept him from hatred and violence.

So Abel's blood cries to our times as it once shrieked in God's ears. We dare not sink to Cain's evil. Our prejudices must be overthrown, and our customs which are based upon prejudice must be re-examined. We must take deliberate action to manifest the grace of the Lord Jesus Christ, the Friend of sinners, for in Christ there is neither east nor west, black nor white, male nor female, bond or free; all are one in him.

Forgive us, our Father, for the many weeks and years in which we have failed to judge ourselves in this particular area. How many times we have glossed over our prejudices and treated them as unimportant trivialities, never realizing that our silence shouts and our refusal to act speaks volumes. Lord, we pray that in this late hour of our history we may be faithful to you in every direction and manifest more fully than we ever have before the saving love that is without prejudice or respect of persons. Thank you for this sharp word from the Scripture to our own hearts, helping us to understand what is happening in our nation today. May we face it in realism and in truth. We ask in Jesus' name. Amen.

3

Too Much, Too Soon

As we work our way through this section of Genesis, we are like explorers who have traced a mighty river to its source and who are now beginning to grasp the character of the land to which they have come. We have already traced the causes of war, crime, and prejudice to their roots in the hearts of men who refuse to be honest before God. In this story of Cain and Abel we have a kind of cameo of history, a microscopic picture of the entire scope of human history. This, of course, is why the Bible is always so contemporary; it deals with elements of human life that never change. The next element we can trace back to its source in Genesis is what is called culture or civilization, and especially the part city life plays in the shaping of human society. This is introduced for us in chapter 4.

Cain knew his wife, and she conceived and bore Enoch; and he built a city, and called the name of the city after the name of his son, Enoch (Gen. 4:17).

We know today that this city actually existed, for archeologists have found the word, Enoch, is the earliest word for city in any human language. In the ancient area of the Tigris and Euphrates rivers the oldest inhabited cities known to man were called "Enoch." In much the same way, people who live near big cities like New York or San Francisco refer to them as "the city." It is interesting that it was Cain who built the first city and thereby turned the family into the state, thus introducing the social and political problems that are screaming at us for solution in this twentieth century. It is very suggestive that the first city was built by a condemned murderer!

The City of God Withheld

Now, it is clear from Revelation 21 that it was ultimately God's intention for men to live in a city. The dream of the city which God intended for man runs throughout the whole of Scripture. We are told in the book of Hebrews that Abraham "looked forward to the city which has foundations, whose builder and maker is God" (Heb. 11:10). So, from the earliest dawn of history, men were looking to the coming of a city. You will find references to it in the Psalms and other places. But everywhere in Scripture a contrast is drawn between the city of God and the cities of men.

God withholds his city and it has not come even yet. He withholds it for a very good reason: he is waiting until men are ready to live in a city. God first goes about solving the fundamental problem of humanity—its self-will and defiance of authority—and then he puts men together in the close life of a city. But we have reversed that. Man, in his arrogance, has assumed that he is quite able to live in intimate relationship with his fellow man and has clustered together in cities throughout history. The result has been the violence, social injustice, and unending bloodshed which history records.

The supreme mark of fallen man is clearly evident in this passage: he wants everything NOW. That is the trouble with man as he is today; he wants everything right now. Instant luxury. Instant comfort. Instant relief. Everything, now! To accomplish it, man ignores the problem of evil. He treats it as though it were nonexistent, dismissing it with a wave of his hand—and goes ahead to build his city on ground that is already red with the blood of his brother. That is the story of history.

Now the city he builds is certainly a most imposing one. The technical brilliance of man is evident even this early in the history of our race. We can trace some of the development of man's expertise in this next section:

> To Enoch was born Irad; and Irad was the father of Mehujael, and Mehujael the father of Methushael, and Methushael the father of Lamech. And Lamech took two wives; the name of the one was Adah, and the name of the other Zillah. Adah bore Jabal; he was the father of those who dwell in tents and have cattle. His brother's name was Jubal; he was the father of all those who play the lyre and pipe. [It is from this we get our word, jubilee.] Zillah bore Tubalcain; he was the forger of all instruments of bronze and iron. The sister of Tubalcain was Naamah (Gen. 4:18–22).

Even the names here are highly suggestive. As you study the Bible, learn to look up the meaning of Bible names.

Sometimes there are differences of opinion as to what they mean, depending upon the root from which the name was taken, but these names are very significant. Irad, for instance, means "the city of witness," i.e., (in this context) witness to the glory of man. Already the idea of the exaltation of man is coming in and it will culminate soon in the tower of Babel, erected to the glory of man. Mehujael means "smitten of God," which perhaps suggests a rather defiant attitude: "God has smitten, yes, but we're going to make a success of this anyway." Methushael is most contemporary; it means "the death of God." You can see how far back into history *that* idea goes! Lamech means "strong" or "powerful," and again reflects clearly the boasting of man in his fallen state. Jabal means "traveler"; Jubal, "trumpeter"; and Tubalcain, "metalworker" —especially with regard to jewelry and ornamentation.

All this is most remarkable; we have here the ingredients of modern life: travel, music and the arts, the use of metals, the organized political life, and the domestication of animals. All of this is intended for man. Nothing that fallen man longs after was to be denied him as far as God was concerned, but it was to be given when man was ready for it. The whole tragic story of civilization is that man insists on it before he is ready for it. How often in history we have said that the story of some human event was "too little, too late." Here it is obviously "too much, too soon."

The Red Thread

These things look impressive and it is desirable to have comforts, luxuries, and advances, but what this passage so clearly brings before us is that it is all built on shaky ground. I do not think I could put that any better than to quote the words of Helmut Thielicke.[1] In a study on this passage, he says:

> The strange thing is that the closer we come the more clearly we see the red thread that runs like a pulsing, bloody artery through the myriad figures of the world. This motherly earth, on which even the greatest of men walked, on which they erected cities and cathedrals and monuments, has drunk the blood of Abel. And this blood of the murdered and abused appears in stains and rivulets everywhere, including the greatest figures. Cain, the "great brother" and progenitor of mankind, betrays his mysterious presence.
>
> Somewhere in every symphony the tone-figure of death is traceable. Somewhere on every Doric column this mark is to be found. And in every tragedy the lament over injustice and violence rings out.

That is what we are trying to forget. We point boastfully at our great skyscrapers, our manicured gardens, our beautiful public avenues and parks, and say all this is the mark of human ingenuity, human ability. But we cover up and ignore the tragic areas of abuse and privation, of darkness and injustice, of violence and intrigue that go along with man's accomplishment. But see how honest, upright and frank the Scriptures are. They make us face right up to truth. The account goes right on to interject two more elements that must be included in an evaluation of human culture:

> Lamech said to his wives:
> "Adah and Zillah, hear my voice;
> 　you wives of Lamech, hearken to
> 　　what I say:

---

[1] Helmut Thielicke, *How the World Began: Man in the First Chapter of the Bible* (Philadelphia, Pa.: Fortress Press, 1961).

I have slain a man for wounding me,
   a young man for striking me.
If Cain is avenged sevenfold,
   truly Lamech seventy-sevenfold" (Gen. 4:23–24).

In this passage you have the first mention of polygamy in the Bible. Someone has said that polygamy has its own punishment; it means more than one mother-in-law! But perhaps there is not even that here; Lamech may have actually married sisters who had the same mother. It occurred to me that perhaps he was simply trying to do research into the nature and character of womanhood, studying it from A to Z, from Adah to Zillah! If you will forgive me that, we'll come back to the text and note that this marks the unfailing accompaniment of civilization: an open toleration of sexual excess. It traces back to this early Cainite civilization. Man's restlessness, even in that early day, seeks fulfillment in multiple marriages, but to no greater success than the woman of Samaria in our Lord's day or any Hollywood movie idol of today.

The second element that is always present and necessary to acknowledge, if we are going to properly evaluate culture, is reflected in this oldest song in the world. Notice that these verses about Lamech are put into poetic form. They represent an early song, a kind of taunt on Lamech's part, in which he justifies his violence. He boasts to his wives, "Listen to what I have to say: I have slain a man for wounding me." Evidently, a young man had assaulted him and, in self-defense, he claims, "I slew him." He boasts of this to his wives and justifies it, reasoning that if God would avenge Cain sevenfold, although he had taken the life of his brother in cold blood, then surely, "I will be avenged seventy-sevenfold for having acted in self-defense." Here we have the first clear instance of a pattern that has repeated itself a thousand times over in human history: the justifying of violence and murder on the ground of the protection of rights.

There is a picture of civilization: Technical brilliance, producing comforts and luxuries; the substitution of the state for the family; the trend toward urban over rural life; the increasing toleration of sexual excess; and the passionate vindication of violence on the grounds of the protection of rights. Sound familiar? Human nature has not changed one iota in the ten thousand years of history recorded since Cain. Listen to this plaint from a fed-up adult:

> Our youth now loves luxuries. They have bad manners, contempt for authority. They show disrespect for elders and they love to chatter instead of exercise. Children are now tyrants, not the servants, of their households. They no longer rise when elders enter the room. They contradict their parents, chatter before company, gobble up their food, and tyrannize their teachers.

So said Socrates, 425 B.C.! Well, what is the problem? It all comes down to this clamant cry of the human heart to have everything now. Men do not want to wait for anything. They do not want to face the fact that perhaps they are not ready yet, that certain changes need to take place in themselves first before they are ready to move into close companionship with one another and live together. It is a refusal to acknowledge the basic problem of human life —the self-centered heart.

Cleansing First

This attitude is manifest in the superficiality of our lives—the fact that we make trivial things sound like they are horribly important. Have you been listening to the toothpaste ads on the TV recently? If you believed the ad, you would think a certain brand of toothpaste could change your whole life. Those ads are intended to be taken in at least a quasi-serious way. But the things that do change life we treat as mere trivia—only for religious people, those few who can't keep their minds off the mystical. They are the ones to whom a true change of life, a born-again experience makes its appeal. How clearly the Scripture puts its finger on the problem of human life— the refusal of human beings to be healed first before they claim the blessings God intends for the race. The cleansing of grace must come first, and then the seeking of God's city.

A father told me recently of the struggles of his son. It was the old, old story of the prodigal son who felt that what his father taught and believed was boring, uninteresting, and useless. Life made its adventurous appeal to him, and he succumbed to the lure of new things and exciting adventures and relationships and refused to stay with his family. He got involved with drugs, bad women, and evil friends, and finally, almost wrecked in health and broken in spirit, he was so tortured and tormented within that he was on the verge of suicide. He realized what was happening to him and, at the last moment repented, came back, and found peace of heart and grace in his father's house. The father said to me, "I don't know why it is that he had to learn the hard way." Well, why is it? It is because men refuse to face the facts about their fallen humanity. For those who refuse to face facts, there is no other way to learn than by hard experience; the grinding tribulation and tumult of having to live with facts we will not recognize.

Another Workman

But this is not necessary. Even this early in the human race it was not necessary. God has another plan ready.

> And Adam knew his wife again, and she bore a son and called his name Seth, for she said, "God has appointed for me another child instead of Abel, for Cain slew him." To Seth also a son was born, and he called his name Enosh. At that time men began to call upon the name of the Lord (Gen. 4:25–26).

Once again these names tell us something. Seth means "appointed." Eve said, "I will call him 'Appointed' because God has appointed another son to take the place of Abel." When the man of faith is taken out of the world, God's work does not end; he raises up another. I have been greatly impressed by the epitaph on the tomb of John Wesley in Westminster Abbey in London. I stood before it some years ago, and read, "God buries His workman, but He carries on His work." So here, too, the work of God is going forward; he appoints another son, another man. The name of Seth's son was Enosh, which means "mortal." The idea here is that in the midst of this Cainite civilization, with its proud refusal to recognize the cancer eating away at the heart of humanity and its desire to achieve on a false basis the luxuries and comforts that God intends, there were yet those who recognized their mortality, and, thus, their dependence upon God. There were those who took God's appointed way and, as the account goes on to say, "they began to call upon the name of the Lord." They recognized that God must heal the heart before we properly have the things that our urges cry out for; that the cancer within us must be dealt with before we can begin to live.

This has been the story of the Scriptures from beginning to end. All the way through, the Scriptures have been at pains to point out to us that there are only two ways to live. Jesus said so, did he not? There is the broad way, which many are taking, which looks so logical but lead to destruction, and there is the narrow, which begins at the point where an individual stands alone before God and must make a decision—the narrow way that leads to life as God intended life to be lived.

Which way are you taking? Are you lured by the siren call of the world, with its appeal to luxury, comfort, ease, achievement, and acquisitiveness? It is not that Christians cannot use these things. The Apostle Paul tells us we are "to use but not abuse" the things of the world. But throughout the Scriptures we are warned, "Love not the things of the world, neither the things that are in the world." Do not make these the center around which you build your life. If these are all-important to you, you are doomed. You will not find life. Jesus said if you try to save your life on these terms, you will lose it. But if you lose your life for his sake, you will save it.

Let God heal the sickness of the human heart with its hunger for self-centeredness, self-exaltation, its desire always to be the center of attention; let God heal that through the working of the gospel, through the grace of the Lord Jesus Christ. Then you can begin to live. It is the way that leads to life. It may be that this life will not include in it luxuries and comforts, but they are down the line somewhere. God has these in mind for all his people. All that the heart hungers after will ultimately be supplied in Jesus Christ. This is why the Apostle Paul cries, "For all things are yours, whether Paul or Apollos or Cephas or the world or life or death or the present or the future, all are yours; and you are Christ's; and Christ is

God's" (1 Cor. 3:21–23). But they are only available to those who begin with the healing of the heart and the cleansing of the life in Jesus Christ.

How foolish we have been, our Father, to try to satisfy our hearts with these empty things of culture and civilization. How foolish we have been to think that a man who is made to be satisfied by God shall ever find heart satisfaction in anything else. How often history has taught us the lesson that those who try to satisfy themselves with something less will end up by repudiating that thing itself, and finding life nothing but a weary desolation of spirit. How long, Father, before we begin to believe you? How long before we begin to take seriously the truth you have told us out of love for us, and turn from setting these secondary things first in our lives. Teach us to make life count, not now but for eternity, that we might enter into life as you intended it to be lived. We pray in your name, Amen.

Genesis 5:1–27

4

Adam's Book

In Genesis 5 we come to the first of the familiar genealogies of Scripture. These genealogies have proved to be
a stumbling block to many who seek to read through the
Bible. They start well, but when they get to a desert of
genealogies they give up their reading. These genealogies
are somewhat difficult. I am tempted to handle them in
the fashion of the old Scots minister who was reading
from the opening chapter of Matthew. He started reading, "Abraham begat Isaac, and Isaac begat Jacob, and
Jacob begat Judah," and he looked on ahead and saw the
long list to follow and said, "and they kept on begetting
one another all the way down this page and halfway into
the next." But it is a mistake to ignore these genealogies;
a careful examination of them can be surprisingly fruitful.

This one begins with a brief introduction and continues, in a standard formula of presentation, throughout the chapter. Look at the first five verses:

> This is the book of the generations of Adam. When God created man, he made him in the likeness of God. Male and female he created them, and he blessed them and named them Man when they were created. When Adam had lived a hundred and thirty years, he became the father of a son in his own likeness, after his image, and named him Seth. The days of Adam after he became the father of Seth were eight hundred years; and he had other sons and daughters. Thus all the days that Adam lived were nine hundred and thirty years; and he died (Gen. 5:1–5).

Now, it is important that we take careful note of the title of this chapter. The phrase, "This is the book of the generations of" occurs only one other place in Scripture. Perhaps you have already guessed that it occurs the second time at the opening of the New Testament in the first verse of Matthew, "This is the book of the generations of Jesus Christ." Here in Genesis it is, "This is the book of the generations of Adam."

The Story of a Race

We are told here that God created man in the likeness of God. This is a recapitulation of what we have seen before. "Male and female he created them, and he blessed them and named them Man . . ." or literally, he named them "Adam." Notice, he did not name them "the Adamses"; it was "Adam." I think the revisers are quite right in translating this "Man," because it is clear that we have here the story of a race, not merely an individual. There is only one man in the Old Testament and that is

Adam. There is only one in the New Testament, and that is Jesus. There are only two men who have ever lived in history, Adam and Jesus—the first Adam and the last Adam; the first Man and the second Man. Thus these two books are introduced by this same phrase, "The book of the generations of . . ." The phrase does not describe ancestry, but characteristics; it describes the nature of these two men as they develop into a race.

We are further told that it was God who named Adam. When Adam named the animals, it was necessary that he understand their character and their nature in order to choose an appropriate name for them. The name reflected the character. Now it is true that only God understands man, therefore, only God can name man because he is the only one who understands him. This is why we so desperately need the revelation of man that comes from God. It is also why psychology cannot be realistic or accurate unless it takes into account what we read in the Scriptures about man. God knows more about man than man does, because God created and named him.

The first thing said in Adam's book is that Seth was made "in the image and likeness" of his father. He was the exact duplicate of what Adam was, as every son and daughter of Adam has been since. Again, this is why the Bible is so contemporary—it is dealing with us. We find ourselves here because we too are sons and daughters of Adam and share the same characteristics as Seth, the son of Adam, one generation removed. When the account uses this phrase, "in his own likeness, after his image," it is referring to both the hidden, inner pattern of man and the actual outward characteristics. Seth was what Adam was, in both his inner life and his outer life. He was, therefore, a fallen man, as we, by the same descent, are fallen men.

Not a Strict Chronology

There then follows a chronology that continues through the rest of the chapter. There are several factors of great interest in this to which I will call your attention as we run through it. First, it is evident, upon careful study, that this chronology was not intended to be a time schedule. This was Bishop Ussher's mistake. He is the one who is responsible for the date, 4004 B.C., that appears in some of our Bibles as the date of creation. He figured this all out (without the aid of a computer) back in the seventeenth century by using these Bible chronologies. But scholars have since pointed out that this is not what they call a "tight" chronology. It does not trace an unbroken lineage of individuals. Rather, it highlights certain individuals. The son that is mentioned for each man is not necessarily the firstborn son; it says of each of them, "He had other sons and daughters." Out of that family one is selected to be included in this genealogy.

The intent of this genealogy, then, is not to give us a tracing of time. This is underscored by the fact that the versions of this account in other languages have different numbers of years for the people involved. The Septuagint, which is the Greek translation of the Old Testament, has a quite different period of years involved, as does the Syriac Version. The obvious intent of the genealogy is to highlight certain selected names. We will come back to the reason a bit later.

The second factor to note about this account is the exceedingly long period of years these men lived. Most of them lived about nine hundred years. Sometimes, perhaps, we might wish we could imitate them, but at other times we feel they were the most cursed of individuals to have to live that long. But the record remains and has raised a problem for many. Several attempts have been made to explain this account. Certain scholars suggest that what we have here is not individuals, but clans, family groups. The years given would be the length of time that family group held together as a single unit, much as the clans of Scotland have. But this is very difficult because it is clear that several of these names clearly refer to individuals. Enoch, for instance, "walked with God." That cannot refer to a clan; but to an individual. Seth, the son of Adam, is also clearly an individual.

Five-Year-Old Father?

Others seek to explain this longevity by taking the years as lunar months; i.e., each "year" would approximate our modern month. If you figure out these men's ages on that basis, it does come out rather interestingly in the upper limits. It would make Methuselah probably about eighty-five or ninety years old when he died, which would destroy his record as the man who lived the longest. But at the lower limits this system becomes absurd. It would mean that Seth became the father of Enosh when he was five years old, which is most remarkable. Some of the miracles required by these explanations are far more incredible than simply to take the account as it appears.

We must conclude, then, that this passage indicates that conditions on earth were widely different before the flood. Earlier chapters in Genesis have suggested the same. It was doubtless true that men lived much longer before the flood than they do today. There have been a number of interesting scientific suggestions made as to why this is true, such as the presence of a canopy of ice or vapor that would shield the earth from harmful rays and create hothouse conditions even at the poles. But it is highly probable that God intended man to live approximately a thousand years before a change took place that would introduce him to a different mode of existence. Of course, all this was changed by the flood.

The third factor that is of great interest is the repeated occurrence throughout this account of the phrase, "and he died." Every individual's entry ends with this phrase: "And he died," "and he died," "and he died," like the tolling of a great bell resounding throughout the passage. Eight times it is recorded, "and he died," contradicting the lie of Satan in the garden when he said to Eve, "If you eat of this fruit you will not die." But here is the factual record. Everyone who came along lived so many years and then he died (except Enoch, whom we will come to in a moment).

This suggests also that all the forms of death, as we know them today, prevailed then. There was physical death, but there are plenty of ways to die. There were also the incipient forms of death that we recognize in our lives today, such as malice, jealousy, hatred, meaninglessness, despair, and emptiness. All these are forms of death—in other words, the absence of life, as God intended life to be. Life before the flood was very much like it is today: a generation seeking after comfort and luxury, brilliant in its technological achievements, banding together in cities and thus creating an artificial form of life, but experiencing hatred, violence, emptiness, and despair.

But now we come to one exception to the tolling of the bell of death—one man of whom it is not said, "and he died." This is evidently the highlight of this chapter, the reason why all this is given to us:

When Enoch had lived sixty-five years, he became the father of Methuselah. Enoch walked with God after the birth of Methuselah three hundred years, and had other sons and daughters. Thus all the days of Enoch were three hundred and sixty-five years. Enoch walked with God; and he was not, for God took him (Gen. 5:21–24).

All of a sudden our interest is stimulated. The whole passage rolls on almost like a movie film until it abruptly stops and focuses on one man. Instead of saying, "and he died," it says, "and he was not, for God took him." The book of Hebrews, in the eleventh chapter, recounts the story of Enoch and tells us that this phrase, "and he was not, for God took him," means that he was "taken up (or translated) so that he should not see death." In other words, here is one of only two men in all history who never died. Enoch is one; Elijah is the other. Enoch did not see death but he was taken up.

Too Far to Go Back

Twice this account says that before he was taken up he walked with God. I love the story of the little girl who was telling her mother the story of Enoch. She said, "Enoch used to take long walks with God. One day he walked so far God said, 'It's too far to go back; come on home with me.'" That is what happened to Enoch. Obviously, the intent of this passage is to focus our attention on this phrase, "he walked with God." What does it mean to walk with God? Here is a man who, in the midst of a brilliant but godless generation, walked with God. What does it mean? Well, it is exactly the same today as it was then. To walk with God is accomplished now in exactly the same way. Enoch did not literally walk with God; this is unquestionably a figurative expression, but a figurative walk involves the same thing today as it did then.

First, it means he went in the same direction God went.

He was moving the way God was going. God is forever moving in human history. He is moving right now to accomplish certain things in human life, and he has been doing so for centuries. The man who walks with God is the man who knows which way God is going and goes the same way. What way is that? What direction is God moving? Perhaps we cannot indicate it positively, but negatively we can say that God moves always in unswerving hostility against sin. He is opposed to that which destroys and wrecks human life. No matter how good it looks, no matter how attractive it seems or how luridly it is painted, God is against it. And the man who walks with God is the man who walks in unswerving hostility toward sin in his own life and refuses to make up with it or permit it to rule or to reign. That is the first thing in a walk with God.

Second, to walk with someone means to keep in step. You cannot walk with another if you do not keep in step with him. Sooner or later there comes an imbalance, and you will bump into him, or he bumps into you. Therefore, you must keep in step. It is most interesting that in the New Testament a walk is described in just this way. It is a series of steps. A walk is not like moving on one of those endless belts. It is not smooth; it is a repetition of almost falling. Have you ever analyzed your walk? Everytime you take a step you almost fall. You allow your body to go off balance and then you catch yourself with your other leg. Then you shift to that and you almost fall again, only to catch yourself. The man or woman who walks with God lives all the time on the verge of a fall.

That is an adventurous life. It means if God is not there to support and strengthen you, down you go. You are counting on him, depending on him to come through and to keep you steady. That is what a walk with God involves—venturing out, never being satisfied with the status quo, never being content to remain in a quiet state and doing nothing. It is forever moving at the same pace God moves. It means taking a step when God insists. I have discovered in my own life (and see it reflected in many others) a tendency to want to sit down after I have taken a step and rest awhile. We all have felt God pressuring us to do something—take a new step, stop this, start that, or venture out in a new direction—and after God pushes us awhile, we do it. Perhaps we have been resisting for quite awhile before, but then we take the step and we feel good. We have accomplished something. Then God comes along and says, "Now I want you to take another step." And we say, "Oh, no, Lord. I had a hard enough time taking this one. Just leave me alone now for awhile. You walk on for a bit and then come back." But the worst thing that can happen to us is for God to walk on ahead.

He did exactly that with the children of Israel when they came to the edge of the Promised Land. He said, "I want you to walk with me into the land." But they said, "No, not us. You go by yourself, but we're not going." So God said, "All right, then you will wander for forty years in the wilderness until you come back to this same place. I'll leave you alone. If you don't want to go in, you don't have to go in." The terrible thing about God is that he gives us what we want. If we want it badly enough, he will let us have it, and it will be the worst thing that ever happened to us. Enoch was a man who learned to move as God moved, to walk in step with him.

The third thing about a walk is that there was no controversy between them. They were in agreement. "Except two be in agreement, how can they walk together?" asks the Scriptures. There must be no controversy between us if we are going to walk with God, but we must agree with the way he sees things. What changes this makes in our lives! Sometimes there are real struggles as we are corrected in our view of things by the Word of God. But if you want to walk with God, you must see things as he sees them, as Enoch did. For three hundred years he walked with God. This is the same activity to which we are called. We are to "walk as children of light." We are to walk "in the Spirit." We are to walk "worthy of God," through the midst of a godless generation exactly as Enoch did.

No Social Security

But notice that Enoch did not always walk with God. The first sixty-five years of his life was quite another story. Evidently he reflected for sixty-five years the same godless attitude as those around him. You ask, "Well, what started him walking with God, then?" And the answer is given to us here. It was not receiving his Social Security payments when he reached sixty-five, but it was the birth of a son, a boy whom he named Methuselah. The account says so: "Enoch walked with God after the birth of Methuselah three hundred years." So it was the birth of this baby that started him walking with God.

Surely there is more to this than simply the fact that he became a father, although I have noticed that becoming a father has a profound effect upon a young man. It makes him more thoughtful, more serious, gives him a more sober outlook on life. It does have a very beneficial effect. But there is more to it than that, and here it is revealed by the name Enoch gave to his son. Methuselah, is a very interesting name. It means, literally, "His death shall bring it," or, loosely translated, "When he dies, it will come." What will come? The flood! Enoch, we are told in another passage of Scripture, was given a revelation from God. He saw the direction of the divine movement, looked on to the end of the culture, the comforts, and the mechanical marvels of his own day, to the fact that there must come an inevitable judgment on the principle of evil in human life. He saw the certainty of destruction of a world living only to please itself. When he saw it, his baby was born, so, in obedience, evidently to God's word, he named the baby, "When he dies, it will come."

This revelation to Enoch is given in the next-to-the-last book of the Bible. If you want to see what a unit the Bible is, notice how Jude and Revelation tie in with Genesis. In the fourteenth verse of Jude we read, concerning certain godless men who would be present in any age, but especially in the last age:

> It was of these also that Enoch in the seventh generation from Adam prophesied, saying, "Behold, the Lord came with his holy myriads, to execute judgment on all, and to convict all the ungodly of all their deeds of ungodliness which they have committed in such an ungodly way, and of all the harsh things which ungodly sinners have spoken against him." These are grumblers, malcontents, following their own passions, loud-mouthed boasters, flattering people to gain advantage (Jude 14–16).

That was the world of Enoch's day, and Enoch saw the end of it. He saw that the Lord was coming to execute judgment on it. Now I know there are those who take that passage in Jude to refer to the second coming of the Lord Jesus Christ, and in a secondary way it does refer to that. But its primary reference is to the judgment of the flood. Enoch saw the coming of the flood, and he named his child, "When he dies, it will come." If you figure out the chronology of this from the life of Noah who was six hundred years old when the flood came, you will find that the very year that Methuselah died, the flood came. It happened exactly as God had predicted.

969 Years of Grace

But the grace of God is revealed here in the fact that this boy lived longer than any man ever lived, nine hundred and sixty-nine years! That is how long God waited before he fulfilled the threat implied in the boy's name. Can you imagine what a fascination this boy must have been to his family? How they watched him every time he went out? "When he dies, it will come." But God let him live longer than anybody else to reveal the heart and compassion of a God who dislikes to bring judgment but does so because of the moral demands made upon his nature of truth.

Now we see the reason for this table of genealogy. First, it is given to highlight the supreme purpose of revelation, to teach us the possibility and importance of a walk with God. That is what men are called to do, to walk with God. It is the greatest glory that can come to any human being, to learn to walk with and be a friend to God. Enoch was the friend of God. Second, this genealogical table is given to warn us of the day when evil shall ultimately be stopped. God cannot allow human evil to increase endlessly. He restrains it, but when it reaches a certain limit, he judges it. That is the repeated story of history. This is the message of the book of Jude. It happens again and again in history. But, as Paul tells us in 1 Corinthians 10, there is always a way of escape provided.

That way of escape is indicated again in a most fascinating way in this chapter by the meaning of the names listed. There is some difference among authorities as to the meaning of these names, depending upon the root from which they are judged to be taken. But one authority gives an interesting sequence of meanings. The list begins with Seth, which means "Appointed." Enosh, his son, means "Mortal"; and his son, Kenan, means "Sorrow." His son, Mahalalel, means "The Blessed God." He named his boy Jared, which means "Came Down," and his boy, Enoch, means "Teaching." Methuselah, as we saw, means "His death shall bring"; Lamech means "Strength," and Noah, "Comfort." Now put that all together. God has *Appointed* that *Mortal* man shall *Sorrow;* but *The Blessed God Came Down, Teaching* that *His Death Shall Bring Strength* and *Comfort.* Is this book from God?

God has given us each a life to watch just as Methuselah's generation watched his. It is our own life. God has written "Methuselah" on each one of us. "His death shall bring it" or "When he dies, it will come." How far is it till the end of the world for you? When you die; that is the end of the world. That is the end of man's day. Is it fifty years from now, ten, tomorrow? Who knows? But at any moment, when you die it will come.

Is it not foolish how we try to escape the inevitability of the end? Yet everything hangs on that. For us, it will be the end of Adam's book when all that Adam is in us is at an end, and there is nothing more to be reached in it. Then only what Christ has written in us will survive. You have heard the little motto,

> Only one life, 'twill soon be past.
> Only what's done for Christ will last.

That is a pithy expression of what we find in this chapter. In Revelation when John saw the dead standing before God, the books also were opened. What books? I think it was Adam's book and Jesus' book. The book of the generations of Adam and the book of the generations of Jesus Christ.

Now one question lingers: What are you doing today in this godless generation? Are you walking with God? Have you learned to keep step with the Almighty? Have you learned to trust what he says and walk in his direction? That is the only basis for any hope of escaping the judgment of death, as Enoch did. Jesus said, "Because I live, you shall live also. He that believeth in me *shall never die.*" For the believer in Christ, death loses its fearful character and is but a momentary transition into the life God has for you.

Thank you, Father, for helping us to view reality, to see through the tinsel, the glitter, the sham, the illusion of life. How helpful it is to see the possibilities of a walk with you as Enoch walked with you, and to believe you and trust you. Teach us so to walk that we may overcome the world and one day you will say to us, "Come on home; it's too far to go back." We thank you in Jesus' name, Amen.

5

Signs of Collapse

ARNOLD TOYNBEE HAS INDICATED that there have been in the past more than twenty-one different civilizations, each one in turn collapsing and giving way to another. So we should not be at all surprised to find here in this definitive passage of Scripture a description of the signs that accompany the imminent collapse of a civilization.

The Bible, as you know, speaks of "times and seasons" in the affairs of men. "Times" are those major divisions of history which are marked by a special character. The Bible speaks, for instance, of the "times of ignorance," referring to the ages before the coming of Christ when men lived in relative ignorance of God. It speaks again of the "times of the restitution of all things" in the future when God will work out all his purposes and unite all things together in Christ. We use similar language when we speak of the "dark ages," characterized by widespread ignorance and moral darkness. But "seasons" are those divisions of time in which certain events come to the fore. I do not think I can do better than to quote Archbishop Trench from his *Synonyms of the Old Testament* in this respect.

> The "seasons" are the joints of articulations in the times; the critical epoch-making periods, ordained of God, when all that has been slowly, and often without observation, ripening through long ages, is mature and comes to birth in grand decisive events which constitute at once the close of one period and the commencement of another.

Remember that Jesus said to his disciples after his resurrection, "the times and seasons are not for you to know." They will unfold as history goes on its way, but we cannot predict when they will occur in the span of time.

It is very important that we recognize these divisions when they do occur, and especially to understand what our Lord meant when he said, "As were the days of Noah, so will be the coming of the Son of man" (Matt. 24:37). Now we are studying the days of Noah. Our Lord linked these two epochs together and said that one is the parallel of the other. If we are living in the days immediately preceding the return of Jesus Christ, we shall find conditions in our day similar to the days of Noah. So in Genesis 6, we have the real story behind the headlines of history. Here we find three steps traced for us that mark the signs of imminent collapse of a civilization.

Mysterious Invasion

The first one is given to us in verses 1 through 4, where we have the account of a demonic invasion:

When men began to multiply on the face of the ground, and daughters were born to them, the sons of God saw that the daughters of men were fair; and they took to wife such of them as they chose. Then the Lord said, "My spirit shall not abide in man for ever, for he is flesh, but his days shall be a hundred and twenty years." The Nephilim were on the earth in those days, and also afterward, when the sons of God came in to the daughters of men, and they bore children to them. These were the mighty men that were of old, the men of renown" (Gen. 6:1–4).

Interest immediately focuses on the question: Who were these sons of God? Why is this account suddenly interjected into the story of mankind? One suggestion that we must take note of is that here we have the blending of two lines—the line of Cain and the line of Seth (which have been followed briefly in previous chapters), and that here is the intermarriage between these two lines, that of the godly (the line of Seth), and the ungodly (the line of Cain). But there are several severe objections to this idea. One, of course, is that this would make the line of Cain the "sons of God," and that hardly seems fitting in view of the biblical picture of the character of Cain and his descendants. It would be much more likely for that description to be applied to the sons of Seth. Then, too, it appears that the ungodly have only sons, while the godly have only daughters. Now that is a perfectly acceptable view as far as I am concerned, since I have four daughters. But it hardly seems possible to take it seriously; it is all too clear that this theory does not take account of all the factors.

There is an alternative view that takes note of the fact that in Scripture it is only by a specific divine act of creation that any being can be termed a son of God. God is a Spirit and man is flesh, and in the New Testament we are told that "that which is born of the flesh is flesh, but that which is born of the Spirit is spirit." So you cannot have men of flesh termed "sons of God" without a divine creative act being performed. In the New Testament Adam is called a son of God because he is the direct result of divine creation, and Jesus Christ is called the Son of God because he is eternally begotten of the Father. Believers are also called sons of God because they are born again by faith in Jesus Christ in a divine creative act. Finally, in the Bible angels are called sons of God for they came directly from the creating hand of God and are not reproduced sexually as men are. It is interesting that in the Old Testament every other use of "sons of God" refers to the angels. You will find in the book of Job, for instance, that the angels are called sons of God.

Now we learn from Jude and Peter in the New Testament that there was a fall of the angels, and the time of that fall is given as "the days of Noah." There are two very interesting passages that link up with Genesis 6. In 1 Peter 3, we have a passage that has been a puzzle to many but which applies directly to this account. Peter says of Jesus that he went "in the spirit" and preached to "the spirits in prison." Now there has been much controversy as to what this means. Some have thought it means that Jesus descended into hell and preached to the spirits in hell during the three days between his crucifixion and resurrection. Personally, I do not ascribe to that theory at all. I think it means that through the Spirit Jesus preached in the days of Noah, speaking in the person of Noah. Noah, we are told, was "a preacher of righteousness," and the Spirit of Christ preached through him.

But the passage goes on to say that the ones preached to are now spirits in prison:

. . . who formerly did not obey, when God's patience waited in the days of Noah, during the building of the ark, in which a few, that is, eight persons, were saved through water (1 Pet. 3:20).

Also in 2 Peter 2:4, Peter recounts a fall of the angels:

For if God did not spare the angels when they sinned, but cast them into hell and committed them to pits of nether gloom to be kept until the judgment; if he did not spare the ancient world, but preserved Noah . . . (2 Pet. 2:4–5).

Note that he links this fall with the days of Noah. Then in the book of Jude we have another reference to this event:

And the angels that did not keep their own position but left their proper dwelling have been kept by him in eternal chains in the nether gloom until the judgment of the great day; just as Sodom and Gomorrah and the surrounding cities, which *likewise* acted immorally and indulged in unnatural lust, serve as an example by undergoing a punishment of eternal fire (Jude 6–7).

There Jude gives us the nature of the sin of the angels. He said it was like that of Sodom and Gomorrah; it was "unnatural lust." This, you can see, is directly in parallel with the statement in Genesis 6, that the "sons of God" came in to the daughters of men and married them, taking wives as they chose. This is evidently regarded in the Scriptures as an unnatural act. Thus we have the picture of fallen angels joining in sexual intercourse with the daughters of men and producing a strange race.

Improper Dwelling

There have been those who object to this idea by pointing out that Jesus said that angels are sexless. In Matthew
22:30 he does say that those who are in the resurrection
"will neither marry nor be given in marriage, but are like
the angels in heaven." It must be noted, however, that
he is speaking here of angels *"in heaven,"* as opposed to
angels in hell. Some have suggested that perhaps there was
a time when angels did have sexual powers, and this of
course would permit the kind of a thing recorded here.
However, it seems more likely that the explanation is
given to us by Jude when he says of these angels that they
"left their proper dwelling" and presumably took up im-
proper dwelling places. Now, bodies in Scripture are called
dwelling places. This very term Jude uses is found elsewhere in Scripture to apply to the body. Its use here implies that the angels took up residence where they did not
belong. The same thing is described in the New Testament in the days of our Lord—the many cases of demonic
possession recorded so frequently in the pages of the Gospels. Evil spirits and fallen angels possessed the bodies
of men, and these demon-possessed men married women
and produced a race of strange beings called here in Genesis 6, the Nephilim. They were a race of giants. The word,
Nephilim, supports this whole idea, because it means "the
fallen ones."

All this strongly suggests that demonic possession has
the ability to affect genetic structure. The chromosomes
are changed so that the progeny are markedly different; a
sort of mutation takes place, and the result is a pronounced
change in the children of such a union. We know today
that LSD has this kind of an effect upon the genetic struc-

ture. Chromosomatic changes take place, and children can be malformed and mentally deficient because of the use of LSD by their parents. It is interesting that in the book of Revelation drugs are linked with demonism and there is some indication that drugs are a means by which the human spirit is opened up to the control of demonic beings (Rev. 9:21). The May 3, 1968, issue of *Time* magazine reported a new theory to the effect that "a genetic abnormality may predispose a man to antisocial behavior, including crimes of violence . . ." A normal male baby has an XY chromosome pattern, but occasionally one is found with an XYY pattern. According to an all-woman team of researchers in Scotland this "May be a supermale, overaggressive and potentially criminal." It was further noted that "the XYY (males) averaged 6 ft. 1 inch tall, whereas the average for others (tested) was 5 ft. 7 inches."

It is clear that the result of this union of demon-possessed men with women was a race of mighty men, "men of renown." Here, I think, is the explanation for the mythological stories of demi-gods—half man and half god—such as Hercules. Mythology is no mere invention of the mind of man; it grows out of the traditions, memories, and legends which were a corruption and perversion of primitive truths.

We are further told in this passage that this occurred "also afterward." This "also afterward" means that after the flood a similar incursion of demonic beings took place. This second invasion resulted in the presence in the land of Canaan of certain gigantic races which are called Canaanites. Perhaps you have stumbled over those long lists of "ites" in the Old Testament and are familiar with these various races—the Jebusites, the Geshurites, the Hittites, etc. All of these are divisions of the Nephilim (they are also called The Rephaim in the Old Testament) who were already there when Abraham came to the promised land. They represent an attempt on the part of demonic powers to derail the divine program of bringing a Redeemer into the world through the human race.

It is interesting that archeologists have now discovered the giant cities of Bashan, and they confirm the fact that races of gigantic beings did exist in this area whose beds are ten, eleven, or twelve feet long. (They had king-size beds in those days, because the kings were really that big). It was these people that the Israelites were commanded to exterminate completely. They were to wipe these giant cities off the face of the earth, to exterminate the whole populace and their animals.

Immediately when this invasion of demonic powers into mankind takes place, notice that God, in his governing grace, limits it:

> Then the Lord said, "My spirit shall not abide in man for ever, for he is flesh, but his days shall be a hundred and twenty years" (Gen. 6:3).

That is sometimes regarded as a reference to the length of life of man before the flood, but in this context I think it is clear that it means, rather, the number of years before the flood, the length of time in which God would permit this kind of thing to go on in human society. The one thing the Bible makes clear everywhere is that God controls human society; he restrains demonic forces and only permits them to operate to a limited degree and for a limited period of time. The idea here, I believe, is that God marked off a hundred and twenty years before the flood, which would be the time when Noah would be permitted to preach the grace of God and extend an invitation to the people of his day to turn from their wicked ways and receive the promise of salvation. Peter confirms this in his first letter when he says that Noah was a preacher of godliness, of righteousness. But the people refused to hear his word during the one hundred and twenty years of the preaching of grace.

Dr. Charles Malik, who was for a long time President of the United Nations and Delegate from Lebanon, once said, "We are still living, as the Germans say *zwischen den zeiten* (between the times) when demonic forces can quickly soar very high and can take possession of the world in very short order." There is a word from a world statesman declaring what the Bible affirms, that demonic forces are at work in human society. The first mark of an imminent collapse of civilization is this appearance of demonic powers which manifest themselves primarily in open and unchecked wickedness.

Enmity Against God

Now we see that wickedness is the second mark given to us in the first part of verse 5, "The Lord saw that the wickedness of man was great in the earth." Unusually intense (that is the meaning of "great") and very widespread (in the earth) wickedness—that is the second mark. The whole world of that day was involved in this. This wickedness is described in detail in various portions of Scripture. Wickedness is always the absence of the life of God at work in human society. It is opposed to the things of God. Perhaps the most vivid, most accurate, and detailed description of wickedness given to us in the New Testament is in the book of Galatians, where the Apostle Paul describes the works of the flesh. It is the flesh that is "enmity against God" and produces wickedness. He says,

Now the works of the flesh are plain [i.e., they are easy to identify; they are obvious]: immorality, impurity, licentiousness [notice how he begins on the sexual level], idolatry, sorcery [witchcraft, or anything to do with the occult], enmity, strife, jealousy, anger, selfishness, dissension, party spirit, envy, drunkenness, carousing, and the like (Gal. 5:19–21).

That is wickedness. It is very noteworthy that in every listing of wickedness you will find the sexual aspects listed first. Paul, in tracing the decline and fall of a society in the first chapter of Romans, speaks of one of the signs of imminent collapse as the turning of men to unnatural lusts with other men, and women to unnatural lusts with other women. The second mark, then, is a widespread and unusually intense manifestation of sexual wickedness; not sporadic but continuous; not localized, but everywhere. Naturally, there have been occurrences of this sort in every civilization at some time. But here, it has a double character; it is continuous and is everywhere present.

Now in the second half of that same verse we have the third mark of the imminent collapse of civilization. It is what Moses calls evil, or debased imaginations, "The Lord saw . . . that every imagination of the thoughts of his heart was only evil continually."

The outward wickedness rested upon a deeper corruption within. The "imaginations of the heart" are the desires and urges for ever more stimulating experiences, what Paul calls in Ephesians "deceitful lusts." In modern parlance, we say "kicks," something that appears to satisfy certain inner urges for excitement. This urge for "kicks" constitutes debased imaginations and finds expression in any society through the creative arts, which depend upon imagination for their motivation and expression—literature, art, and drama. It is most significant that more and more today we are finding this area given over to the expression of the salacious, the lewd, and the sensual. I heard of a teacher in public school who refused to teach literature anymore because of the salacious content of what he had to teach. He simply gave up his training and professional background in order to avoid having to teach this kind of stuff.

All of this is summed up for us in two words in verse 11, "Now the earth was *corrupt* in God's sight, and the earth was filled with *violence*." Corruption is inward pollution, the polluting of the mind, the heart, the imagination, the inner nature. The result is outward destructiveness, the outbreak of cruelty and violence on every side. There you have the marks of an impending collapse of civilization. Rather sobering, is it not? When civilization reaches this stage, the Bible clearly implies that judgment by divine fiat is certain. We read on:

> And the Lord was sorry that he had made man on the earth, and it grieved him to his heart. So the Lord said, "I will blot out man whom I have created from the face of the ground, man and beast and creeping things and birds of the air, for I am sorry that I have made them." But Noah found favor in the eyes of the Lord (Gen. 6:6–8).

When the account says, "The Lord was sorry," it is really, "God repented." But we know from other Scriptures that it is impossible for God to repent. He does not change his mind like man does. This is a powerful figure to express in a vivid way the anger and determination of God. When society reaches this stage of dissolution and deterioration, God's anger burns. It appears that he has changed his mind completely even though he is but acting on principles that are entirely consistent with his own being.

Yet, in the midst of this, we read that it grieved him, and grief is always the activity of love. What we finite human beings do not understand is that God's love and wrath are exactly the same thing. They are two sides of the same coin. What entrances us and warms us about God and draws us to him is love, the manifestation of his total being. He is the God of love, who loves regardless of merit. This is what attracts us. But it is because we respond that he appears to us in that way. To those who reject his love, the same quality in God becomes wrath and it seems to be a wall of fire, burning and consuming everything. We can see this also in ourselves; it is our love that causes us to be angry at anything which injures what we love. If you injure a child in the mother's presence, watch her love flame out in anger against you. Thus we have here clearly described a time when man, in his rejection of God, passes beyond the place of seeing God as love and begins to experience his love as wrath.

Along with mankind goes the whole creation in judgment. Why? Because the creation is linked with man. The animals were made for man. So when man goes, the animals must go as well. But always there is the shining of grace: "But Noah found favor [or literally, grace] in the eyes of the Lord."

God was calling throughout this whole age, just as he is calling in our age today, and pleads with men to turn from their ways, to resist the widespread lie of Satan. One man and his family turned and found grace in God's sight. He did not deserve it, and he could equally have turned and gone the other way, but he responded to the wooing and pleading of God and found grace in his sight.

Now bring this down to this twentieth-century hour and draw the parallel between the days of Noah and the days in which we live. You can see it plainly everywhere.

We must remember that if we are delivered from the wrath to come, if we escape the judging hand of God upon society, it is not because of anything we have done; it is the manifestation of God's grace. Remember the Christian who saw a drunkard staggering down the street wallowing in his own vomit and turned to his friend to say, "There but for the grace of God, go I." We can all say that. What has kept us? What has brought us to the truth? Was it any goodness on our part? No, it is God's grace. It is that he loved us and called us, he wooed us and won us, seeking us out and, through many influences upon us, bringing us at last to see that the age in which we live is an age under the bondage of a lie. He has opened our eyes, partially at least, to the truth, till we have turned to the Lord Jesus and rested under the grace of God. While our age deteriorates as other ages have done before us, and our civilization nears the point of utter collapse, we can thank God that we have been snatched away as brands from the burning, like Noah and his family, if our hearts are responsive to the appeal of God's grace.

Our Father, we thank you for this honest, searching look at our world today. How true the statement of Jesus is, that "as it was in the days of Noah, so shall it be also in the days of the coming of the Son of Man." We believe that we can recognize the signs that confirm the near coming of our Lord Jesus Christ and the imminent collapse of what we call civilization in this twentieth-century hour. Grant to us then that we may live as those who see the light, and not as men in the darkness; that we no longer give ourselves to shortsighted programs and the seeking of pleasures and luxuries for ourselves, but grant that we may be available instruments of your grace to live in an hour which is under the judgment of your hand. We ask in Jesus' name, Amen.

6

The Way of Escape

As WE COME to the subject of the flood, a dozen questions come rushing to our minds. Did the flood really occur? How widespread was it? Was it universal, or only partial? Was there really an ark, and was it large enough to hold all the animals? Where did all the water come from? These questions and others like them seek an answer when we come to this subject.

But we must note right away that Scripture does not focus on these things. We shall try to answer these questions as we go along, but we must not miss the emphasis of Scripture. Hollywood would undoubtedly turn this story of Noah and the flood into an extravaganza of terror. The cameras would zoom in on weeping mothers, crazed animals, crashing buildings, and other phantasies of horror. But in Scripture the great flood is not the center of attention; it is the story of one man and his family. This is not an account of world disaster, essentially; it is the story of survival. Why did Noah survive the flood? That is the supreme question; not why or how did the flood occur, but why did one man and his family survive? Thus the account of the flood opens with an answer to that question:

These are the generations of Noah. Noah was a righteous man, blameless in his generation; Noah walked with God. And Noah had three sons, Shem, Ham, and Japheth (Gen. 6:9–10).

Here is the sort of man whom God reckons worthy to survive a world disaster. Let us remind ourselves at this point of the words of Jesus, "As were the days of Noah, so will be the coming of the Son of man." Every one is well aware of the imminent possibility of worldwide destruction that hangs over our present society. We know that our human race has come to the place where it is trembling on the verge of self-extinction. The more we go on in time the more the possibility looms and the less likely it seems that we can find some way to escape it. We are living in days similar to the days of Noah, the days before the flood. At such a time the eyes of God are not upon Johannesburg or Paris or Washington or Moscow or Peking. Not that these cities are outside the scope of God's interest, but they represent events which are mere finger exercises in the divine providence. But Scripture tells us, "The eyes of the Lord run to and fro throughout the whole earth, to show his might in behalf of those whose heart is blameless toward him" (2 Chron. 16:9). That is where Scripture focuses its interest. So the center of attention of this whole story is the man Noah and the family that accompanied him into the ark.

The Righteousness of Faith

Three things are given here about Noah that we must note. First, he was said to be righteous. Most of us think of the word "righteous" as meaning "good"; "Noah was good." We are tempted then to say, "Well, that explains everything. God saw that Noah was good, and, therefore, he chose him to be saved. Obviously, you choose the good man to be saved." But that is not what it says. The actual fact is that God made Noah righteous and then he became good. It was because he was first righteous that he became good. God made him righteous because he believed. The book of Hebrews tells us that Noah, by faith, was warned by God of things not yet seen. And he believed God, constructed an ark, thus condemning the world, and became the heir of that righteousness which comes by faith. That is the only kind of righteousness the Bible knows anything about. It is a righteousness which is not a result of our working, not a result of our best efforts put forth to try to please God, but a righteousness which comes by believing God. That is the kind that Noah had.

Once when I was visiting a college fraternity house, a boy asked me what he considered to be a difficult question: "If two men do exactly the same deed, but one of them is a Christian and the other is not, are not the deeds they do equally good in the eyes of God?" My answer, of course, was no. Anticipating that answer, he went on to point out that Christianity must therefore be unrealistic and impractical. It presumes to judge the quality of identical deeds as being different and thus is totally unrealistic. I tried to point out to him that it was he who was being unrealistic, for he was merely judging from the effects the deeds had upon the persons benefited, but he was giving no consideration to the effect the deeds had upon the persons who performed them, or that the motives of the heart would make a considerable difference. I have known many deeds that were good from an external viewpoint, but which were really very evil deeds because of the motive from which they were performed.

We are told that "man looks on the outward appearance, but God looks on the heart," not only in the realm of motive, but also, more precisely, in the realm of the origin of deeds. Who is acting within the individual? God knows that man is incapable of doing anything in himself; he can only give himself to another power to operate through him. God's great question of mankind is: to what power do you give yourself? Jesus said to the rich young ruler, "Only God is good." Therefore the only good deeds in God's sight are those which he himself does. God is interested in the origin of our deeds—whether they are the result of the activity of God in our hearts or some other power. That is the question we are facing concerning Noah. Noah believed God, and because he believed him, God was at work in Noah. Therefore, he was righteous, because only God can be righteous. Noah had received that righteousness which is God's righteousness, not man's; which is imparted not by works but by faith, by believing the word of God.

A Whole Person

Second, we are told that Noah was blameless in his generation. The nearest English equivalent to the Hebrew word translated "blameless" is the word "whole." To borrow from a title of one of Dr. Paul Tournier's books, Noah was "A Whole Person in a Broken World." How descriptive that is of this man. He lived in a world filled with violence, cruelty, and sexual perversions. When these are evident in history, they are always signs and manifestations of inner turmoil, of tensions and frustrations within, of fears, anxieties, worries, wild urges and impulses. In what way, therefore, was Noah blameless? Why was he whole when the rest of society had gone to pieces? He was whole because he was righteous. God always begins at the heart of the matter. Surely this is the problem with society today. Because man refuses the righteousness which God offers by faith, the basis of human operation which he alone can give, man cannot be good. But the man who receives that righteousness becomes good, as Paul makes clear in the opening chapters of Romans. So Noah found the secret of control. He had an inner peace imparted by the indwelling of God, the righteousness which comes by faith. Therefore he was blameless; he was a whole person, well-adjusted, able to handle the situations that came his way, at peace with himself internally.

Third, as a result of the first two factors, he walked with God. This means a daily experience of contact with God. Noah did not look back to his conversion and rely on that as his contact with God. Rather, he was in continual daily communication with God. He talked with God about the building of the ark. Not only did he get the original blueprints from God, but I am sure he discussed with him all the details of just how it was to be constructed. He walked and lived with God from day to day. This is the secret of a man who survives the disaster of his age.

A fourth thing mentioned about Noah here is that he was the head of a family: "Noah had three sons, Shem, Ham, and Japheth." He did not turn aside from the normal enterprises and occupations of life; he was a normal individual. Here is the first of many passages in the Bible which speak of the relationship of a man to his family. It is apparent that through Noah's faith these three also were saved. I do not want to press this unduly, but there are other passages in the New Testament that describe how the faith of the head of a family affects the whole family. I do not mean to imply that Shem, Ham, and Japheth did not also believe in God. I think they did. But the point that is suggested here is that they believed in God primarily because their father did, and that a head of a family exercises a unique relationship and control over the rest of his family in the eyes of God. There is much more that needs to be explored in this respect. Certainly, we Americans have lost many family secrets. We do not understand how families operate. We need again to learn how God views a family and the unique responsibility and control that a head of a family can employ. It was not due to Shem, Ham, and Japheth that they entered the ark; it was because of Noah.

As the account moves from its focus upon this man, who is a picture and prototype of the kind of people who can survive a world disaster, the second major emphasis is upon the character of the age in which he lived.

Now the earth was corrupt in God's sight, and the earth was filled with violence. And God saw the earth, and behold, it was corrupt; for all flesh had corrupted their way upon the earth. And God said to Noah, "I have determined to make an end of all flesh; for the earth is filled with violence through them; behold, I will destroy them with the earth" (Gen. 6:11–13).

We have already seen the detail of this corruption and violence, the inevitable marks in any civilization of an impending disaster. Here is the pattern man follows. Man is by nature and creation a fully dependent being. He must depend upon God for his life, his breath, his activity, his intelligence, his power of choice, and everything he does. He is the most dependent of creatures, even more so than the animals. He lacks even the instincts which animals have. Yet, fallen man denies this most important point of his life and is forever trying to assert his ability to do everything himself. But when man attempts it, he soon has everything in such a terrible state that it can no longer be controlled. He lacks the rationale, the intelligence, the knowledge to control. He deludes himself into thinking that he has the ability to control his life and, as a result, nature (including human nature) goes out of control. The delicate balance of life is tilted beyond the critical point, and then a collapse occurs. This has proved again and again to be true in the history of civilization and, occasionally, as we have in this account, of nature itself. It may well be that the flood was brought about by man's intemperate misuse of elemental forces— he tripped the balance in a delicate scale which brought about the flood.

Poisons Distilled from Gifts

This is right in line with the Apostle Paul's revelation of the way God moves in human affairs. He reveals in Romans, chapter 1, that God gives man over, gives him up, to exercise the folly he insists upon in order that he might see from the results how foolish he has been. Helmut Thielicke, in his book, *How The World Began*, puts it this way:

> The powers of destruction are still present in the midst of creation. The atoms—did not God create them?— need only to be split, the bacteria let loose, hereditary factors monkeyed with, genes tampered with, and poisons

need only to be distilled from the gifts of creation—oh yes, the powers of destruction are still with us and the heavenly ocean is still heaving and surging behind its dams. We live solely by the grace of God, who has fixed the bounds of destruction. The dreadful secret of the world revealed in the first chapters of this old Book is that man is capable of *renouncing* and cutting himself off from this very grace which holds in check the power of destruction.

No sooner does (man) worship his own power—no sooner does he regard flesh or atomic power as his "arm" and surrender to the illusion that he can hold the world in order and balance by military potential and political intelligence (how appropriate that is to this day)—then he has already renounced God's grace and breached the dam that holds the heavenly ocean. When he imagines that he can free men from need and fear by means of the welfare state he is already declaring himself independent of this sustaining grace and pressing the buttons which set off the secret signals of catastrophe.

Above all, when we are people who calmly tolerate the routine business of the church's baptizing, marrying, and burying, but otherwise go on stubbornly worshiping our anxieties and succumbing to prosperity and its self-indulgence and superficiality; when therefore we are people who do not see their neighbor in his need and thus lose our souls, *then* and precisely *then,* we too are playing fast and loose with that grace which guards the dikes of ruin.

And therefore this world, which we think we govern by our own power, may one day come crashing down upon us, because the thing we play with so presumptuously has gotten beyond our control, and because God is not to be mocked. He may suddenly cease to hold the ocean in check and the unleashed elements will sweep us into their vortex.

Those eloquent words describe exactly what happened in the days of Noah. We face the same chilling possibility in our own day.

No Mythical Account

The third emphasis in this account is most timely. God moves immediately to present to us a description of the way of escape. It is found in the description of the ark:

> Make yourself an ark of gopher wood; make rooms in the ark, and cover it inside and out with pitch. This is how you are to make it: the length of the ark three hundred cubits, its breadth fifty cubits, and its height thirty cubits. Make a roof (or window) for the ark, and finish it to a cubit above; and set the door of the ark in its side; make it with lower, second, and third decks (Gen. 6:14–16).

Obviously this is not a mythical account. The instructions that are given here are precise, matter-of-fact, and explicit. This whole account is of that character. There is nothing vague, nothing mythical about it. There *was* an ark and it *did* save Noah and the animals, and all of Scripture is confirmation of that fact. We may discount the rumors that exist that the ark is still somewhere around. Perhaps it may yet be discovered high on the shoulders of Mt. Ararat, for there have been some rather strange accounts of men who have allegedly seen it there. But our faith does not rest upon rumors. We can discount these rumors, at least until they have been established as facts, but the historicity of the ark remains unimpaired. This story of the flood is also supported by flood legends from primitive peoples all over the earth.

But God's way, as we have seen before in these stories in Genesis, is to hide wheels within wheels. Not only was the ark a literal boat which was literally used in that early day to save a civilization, but it is also a symbol or type, pointing to something else. The Apostle Peter hints very strongly that the ark is a type, a shadow, of the Lord Jesus Christ. See how every detail of the ark points in that direction. We are told, first, that it was made of gopher wood. I do not know what gopher wood is and apparently no one does. The nearest guess of Bible scholars is that it is cedar or acacia. But the word gopher is an interesting one. Gopher, and the word, pitch, which occurs in this passage, and also the Hebrew word (used later on in the books of Moses) for atonement, are all from the same basic Hebrew root, which means "to cover." Thus the ark was made from "atonement wood" or "redemption wood" and pitched, made waterproof, with "atonement." This word for atonement speaks of expiation of sin and oneness between God and man. It is the prominent feature of the Bible and its use here hints strongly of the redemptive work of the Lord Jesus who was sent as an ark of safety for the people of God to carry them through the floods of God's judging vengeance.

Furthermore, Noah was told to build rooms in the ark. Now this is the common word for nests, such as bird nests, and it is strongly suggestive that the ark was intended to be not only a place of safety but of rest and comfort. Thus in Jesus Christ we find not only safety against the floods of vengeance, but also rest and comfort. Of further significance are the dimensions of the ark: three hundred cubits long, fifty cubits wide, and thirty cubits high. A cubit is a little short of two feet. This would make the ark something like four hundred and fifty feet long—a very large vessel. No wonder it took almost one hundred and twenty years to construct. It was built on dry land, a long way from any lake or sea, and built in obedience to the command of God and, to be sure, in the face of the mockery of the age in which Noah lived. These dimensions are pointed out by St. Augustine to be "the dimensions of a man." Of course, no man is three hundred cubits long, but Augustine means the ratio between length, height, and width is exactly that of a full-grown man. So again we have a picture of a Man, our ark of safety the Lord Jesus Christ, the second Man, who came to redeem us.

There is also a window in the ark, but it is not placed in the side where Noah can look out upon the destruction around him, but in the top, where he can only look up. If this is a picture of the Lord Jesus Christ, it is suggestive of that upward look which he manifested throughout his lifetime. He took his orders from his Father. His eye was forever fixed upon him. He came to do the will of his Father and walked in obedience to him. He did not take his motivation from that which was occurring around him, but from that which came from above, as he himself said again and again.

Then there is only one door in the ark as there is only one way into Christ, by faith. There is not a door for the elephants and another door for the mice, and another for the insects; they all come in through one door. It is placed in the side of the ark. It is suggestive of the very words of Jesus, "I am the door; if any one enters by me, he will be saved" (Jn. 10:9).

Finally, we are told there were three decks to be built in the ark. Perhaps this is a hint of the humanity of our Lord—body, soul and spirit. The whole man was given up for us. Also there is provision in Christ for the completion of the whole man—body, soul, and spirit; we are to be wholly redeemed in him. It is this ark, then, that is to bear us, as the ark bore Noah, through the flood of judgment that is to come.

Mini-Crises

But I think there is more here. God is not only picturing for us the crisis that comes in history, but also these mini-crises that come in all our lives from time to time. Remember in 1 Corinthians 10:13 the Apostle Paul tells us, "God is faithful, and he will not let you be tempted beyond your strength, but with the temptation will also provide the way of escape [an ark, a place of refuge] that you may be able to endure it." This strikes me as greatly needed in this day. I am occasionally reminded by some that I have not been available when they needed me. They have tried to reach me and could not locate me when they needed help. I always want to be available when anyone really needs help, but I never feel badly when someone tells me that. I know that often that is God's way of turning their eyes away from human help to the only help that is *always* available and which we so frequently fail to avail ourselves of: the way of escape that is in Jesus Christ. This is what he is for. He is a refuge, a place of safety. He is a place of security, or rest and comfort in time of pressure. The whole of Scripture urges us to avail ourselves of him, not some other human being. In the greatest floods and testings of life human help is unavailing anyhow. What real good does it do? We must eventually turn to this ark that is provided for us, our way of escape. I am convinced that more of us would find ourselves living stable, sensible lives in the midst of the most amazing pressures if we would but find our way to the ark of safety, the way of escape which is in Jesus, and take refuge within him in the hour of pressure.

Now the final emphasis of this account is given:

"For behold, I will bring a flood of waters upon the earth, to destroy all flesh in which is the breath of life from under heaven; everything that is on the earth shall die. But I will establish my covenant with you; and you shall come into the ark, you, your sons, your wife, and your sons' wives with you. And of every living thing of all flesh, you shall bring two of every sort into the ark, to keep them alive with you; they shall be male and female. Of the birds according to their kinds, and of the animals according to their kinds, of every creeping thing of the ground according to its kind, two of every sort shall come in to you, to keep them alive. Also take with you every sort of food that is eaten, and store it up; and it shall serve as food for you and for them." Noah did this; he did all that God commanded him (Gen. 6:17–22).

The emphasis here, again, is not upon the extent of the flood; it is upon the fact that when Noah came into the ark, God said to him, "I will make my covenant with you." It was not merely the ark that saved Noah. That was the *means* by which his salvation was accomplished, but what really saved Noah was God's agreement with him. The Word of God, the promise of God; that is what saved him. We too must look beyond the means by which we are saved—the cross and the resurrection—to the great motivation that brought Christ to earth, to the promise of God which underlies everything else and makes covenant with us, a covenant, a new arrangement for living. Whenever you see this word "covenant" in Scripture, do not think of it so much as a contract that God makes with man. Primarily, it is a new basis for life, an arrangement for living. This covenant goes further than simply saving Noah; it is to govern his life and the life of the world after the flood is over. It requires but one attitude on Noah's part—obedience.

His Right to Rule

I bring this out particularly because I am disturbed by the ease with which many people seek to use the Lord Jesus as a Savior to save them from going to hell when they die, but they have no intention of allowing him to govern their lives while they live. But the story of Noah is very clear; it is not merely the fact that God brought Noah into the ark that saved him. Rather, it was that Noah was obedient to and entered into a new arrangement for living. Noah obeyed God; he did all that was commanded. God undertook, therefore, to regulate his life on a totally different basis.

This is what saved Noah, and this is what saves us. It is not the fact that we accept Jesus Christ as our Savior, thus agreeing that we belong to him and will be saved when we die. It is the fact that we have received him as *Lord*. We recognize his rights over us—his right to rule, his right to regulate, his right to command us and our need to obey. The heart is to respond immediately in obedience to all that God commands, as Noah did here. That acknowledgment of Lordship is the basis of salvation. That is the basis on which we not only will survive the disaster that hangs imminently over our age, threatening to strike at any moment, but also the individual disasters of every life that can cut the ground out from beneath the house of life and demolish it, washing away the sands upon which we build.

We must establish our lives upon a rock which cannot be moved, which rests upon the most unshakable thing in all the universe—the Word of God. After all, that is what created the universe. The word of God is the most solid thing there is. There is nothing more dependable than the word of God. When we rest, therefore, upon the word of God, the covenant of God, we rest upon the most certain and sure thing in the universe. "Heaven and earth," Jesus said, "will pass away, but my words will not pass away" (Matt. 24:35).

Thank you, Father, for turning our eyes from transitory and ephemeral things, passing things, to the permanent, the sure, the unshakable. What a restive world we live in. How uncertain and confused is the generation around us. How restless are the voices we hear on every side. But we thank you, Lord, that you turn us to that which remains solid and secure. You invite us to enter the place of safety, the one person who can take us through all that life can throw at us and bring us safely out on the other side, the ark of the Lord Jesus Christ, in whose name we pray, Amen.

7

The End of the Old

As WE CONTINUE with the story of the flood I want to set
this Old Testament account in the light that streams from
a New Testament passage. The Apostle Peter, in his second letter, says that scoffers will appear in the last days
raising doubts about the return of Jesus Christ, and saying, "Where is the promise of his coming?" That is, what
grounds have you to expect this to be fulfilled? The basis
for their scoffing will be that "all things have continued
as they were from the beginning of creation." Their claim
is that Christians have no right to expect a supernatural
intervention of God in the physical operation of the earth.
This is what is called today the theory of uniformitarianism, i.e., the scientific theory that what exists in the
natural realm has been produced by laws that have op-
erated in the past as they are observed today, and that

these have never varied. Certainly much can be explained by this, though not all; yet rigid uniformitarianism is the basis for much of the approach of physical science to the study of the earth today. Peter says that those who argue on this basis deliberately ignore a contrary fact. The essence of science is to deal with facts, but Peter's charge is that those who claim that there can be no supernatural intervention into the affairs of nature have deliberately ignored a fact—the fact of the flood. Here is the way he puts it:

> They deliberately ignore this fact, that by the word of God heavens existed long ago, and an earth was formed out of water and by means of water, through which the world that then existed was deluged with water and perished.

Then he goes on to show how the past points to the future:

> But by the same word the heavens and earth that now exist have been stored up for fire, being kept until the day of judgment and destruction of ungodly men (2 Pet. 3:5–7).

As Christians, who believe that the apostles of our Lord Jesus spoke by divine inspiration and were given a special word of authority about matters beyond human ken, we must read the story of the flood in the light of this declaration. From this word of Peter three things guide us in our study of the flood.

First, this was not an ordinary flood, involving the ordinary forces that produce floods in our day. It involved unusual and distinctive forces which had perhaps never been employed before, and (we have been given great assurance of this in Scripture) are never to be employed again. Second, its effects were literally world-shaking, for the whole structure of the earth was altered by this flood. Third, it points to a future physical disturbance of the earth, this time not by water but by fire. It is clear that the whole point of Peter's argument is that God does intervene dramatically in nature as well as in human affairs. He does so to produce sudden changes which are unanticipated except 'by revelation. He did this before, and he will do it again. As we read chapter 7 of Genesis we must note the parallels that occur between the flood and the judgment which awaits this present world. Peter says the coming judgment will be similar in many ways to the flood, differing only in the agent involved, fire instead of water.

Come into the Ark

Chapter 7 brings before us the basis on which salvation occurs. After all, that is the heart of this whole story in Genesis, as we have already seen. It is not attempting to give us scientific aspects of the flood, although what it says is scientifically accurate. What it is trying to get across is a picture of something which is also happening in your life and mine, involving the important issue of salvation —deliverance from an overwhelming judgment. This is brought out clearly in the first five verses:

Then the Lord said to Noah, "Go into the ark, you and all your household, for I have seen that you are righteous before me in this generation. Take with you seven pairs of all clean animals, the male and his mate; and a pair of the animals that are not clean, the male and his mate; and seven pairs of the birds of the air also, male and female, to keep their kind alive upon the face of all the earth. For in seven days I will send rain upon the earth

forty days and forty nights; and every living thing that
I have made I will blot out from the face of the ground."
And Noah did all that the Lord had commanded him
(Gen. 7:1–5).

This account begins with an invitation; the Revised
Standard Version is certainly wrong in rendering this
word of God to Noah, *"Go* into the ark." The Hebrew
word is, *"Come* into the ark," with the clear implication
that God is waiting in the ark. God will be with Noah in
the ark, so Noah and his family are invited to join him
there. We can hear in this "come," anticipations of the
invitation which the Lord Jesus continually extends to
men. The whole thrust of all that God has to say to men
finds its focus in one invitation. "Come unto me," Jesus
said, "all you that are weary and heavy laden, and I will
give you rest." "If any man thirst, let him come unto me."
That is the word of Christ to men, "Come unto me."

The basis upon which this call was extended to Noah is
given here, "I have seen that you are righteous before me
in this generation." It is important to notice that Noah
was not only righteous, he was *seen* to be righteous. He
not only believed and thus became righteous, but his
subsequent actions demonstrated his belief. He believed
God and, therefore, he obeyed God. You never can say
you believe God unless you obey him, because that is what
belief really is. It is our motivation to obedience.

Noah demonstrated his faith in his day and generation
by constructing an ark in obedience to the word of God,
against the ridicule and contempt of his age. Use your
imagination here to picture the mockery that must have
greeted Noah as he built his ark on the plains, far away
from any adequate river or ocean in which it might float.
Imagine the reaction of his ungodly neighbors to this
queer old saint, as he spent his resources and involved the

labor of his sons as well to build the ark. How they must have poked fun at him and the stories he told of a coming judgment. And he was building it for animals, as well as men! You can imagine what was said.

It was not easy for Noah to obey God. There were no physical signs of coming judgment. The skies were clear overhead, the sun was rising and setting as it had for generations. As Jesus said, "Men were marrying and giving in marriage." Business was going on as usual. Yet Noah believed God and constructed an ark, thus condemning the world.

Is that not the test of faith today, as it is in any age? The thrust of Scripture is always in this direction. Christians are not to be conformed to this world; they are to be different in their attitude and their reactions. The demonstration of our faith comes right at this point. How much have we believed God? It will be evident in the way we refuse to reflect the deluded attitudes of the world around us, in how we refuse to give way to a hungering after things, the urge for materialistic gain, and in the way we refuse to retaliate when someone abuses us or takes advantage of us. It will be seen in the way we refuse to lie to one another, even with so-called "white lies," which are the blackest of all, because they mean we do not love people enough to tell them the truth. Here is the test. Noah was seen to be righteous; his faith was genuine, and, therefore, he was called into the ark.

The Animals Belong

Notice that this salvation was linked with the animal creation. It is wonderfully comforting to me to realize that God cares for cats and dogs and elephants and wrens—all the animals, the birds, and the insects—the whole world of nature. We sing of it sometimes in a hymn that has unusual claim upon our affections. I sense a response in the hearts of God's people every time we sing, "Fairest Lord Jesus, ruler of all nature." I love that picture. There at the manger scene were the ox, the ass, and the sheep. The angels did not say, "Drive those animals out of here." They belonged in the picture, for God is Lord of all the earth—all the things of earth are his, and he cares for them. As Jesus said, "Not even a sparrow falls to the ground without your Father's will" (Matt. 10:29). I don't know how many times I have been helped to belief by that simple rhyme you may have on your walls at home:

> Said the Robin to the Sparrow,
> "I would really like to know
> Why these anxious human beings
> Rush about and worry so?"
>
> Said the Sparrow to the Robin,
> "Friend, I think that it must be
> That they have no Heavenly Father
> Such as cares for you and me."

We have here also the divisions between clean and unclean animals. It is interesting that this occurred and is recognized long before the Law was ever given. This distinction is not only a part of the Law of Moses but was made as early as the days of the flood. It is a distinction which is essentially temporary and artificial. Actually, as the New Testament makes clear, there are no clean and unclean animals, for all the creatures of God are clean. But this artificial distinction was drawn in Old Testament days in order to teach men a needed truth, as all these physical things are intended to teach spiritual truth. As soon as the lesson was clearly evident in the work of

Christ, the distinction disappeared. We are not to observe such distinctions today. It was intended to teach, by certain functions of the animals that were designated as clean, corresponding spiritual qualities that God loves; while the absence of those functions in the unclean animals was intended to teach that God disapproved of these in the lives of men. Obviously these seven clean animals were taken into the ark in order to provide the sacrifices which Noah performed as he came out of the ark.

Now the second great thing in this chapter is the thoroughness of the flood:

> Noah was six hundred years old when the flood of waters came upon the earth. And Noah and his sons and his wife and his sons' wives with him went into the ark, to escape the waters of the flood. Of clean animals, and of animals that are not clean, and of birds, and of everything that creeps on the ground, two and two, male and female, went into the ark with Noah, as God had commanded Noah. And after seven days the waters of the flood came upon the earth.
> In the six hundredth year of Noah's life, in the second month, on the seventeenth day of the month, on that day all the fountains of the great deep burst forth, and the windows of the heavens were opened. And rain fell upon the earth forty days and forty nights (Gen. 7:6–12).

It is difficult to see how anyone could read this as a myth; it has such precision about it. This eleventh verse seems to be copied right out of the log of the good ship Grace: "In the six hundredth year of Noah's life, in the second month, on the seventeenth day of the month . . ." The precise day upon which the rains came is recorded here by Moses. They came on a precisely appointed day in the calendar of God, a day which was chosen in relationship to the man of God. It was in the six hundredth year of Noah's life that the flood came. What does that suggest? Well, it suggests that this is the way God appoints his calendar. Events occur not on arbitrary dates—June 12th, or March 21st—isolated from the needs and development of men, but rather, on the basis of what has happened or not happened in the life of a certain person or people. When the chosen ones have reached a certain prescribed point, then another event takes place. God sets up his datebook by the progress of the people of God. When Noah's appointed task was completed, then the flood descended.

We see this also in the New Testament. There are certain indications there that when the church fulfills its appointed task and comes to the place of understanding upon which God has determined, then it will be removed in the twinkling of an eye and judgment will come. This is what Peter means in his second letter about "hastening the day of God" (2 Pet. 3:12). He says that the way people live will determine how soon this event will occur. You can "hasten the coming of the day of God." Remember that the Apostle Paul, preaching to the Athenians, said: "God has fixed a day on which he will judge the world in righteousness . . . and of this he has given assurance to all men by raising him [Christ] from the dead" (Acts 17:31). That is the guarantee that the day which has been appointed is linked to the people of God, just as Noah's appointed day was.

Possible Explanations

Notice also in this account that earth and all its peoples were involved. The very structure of the earth seems to have been altered. "On that day all the fountains of the great deep burst forth, and the windows of the heavens were opened" (Gen. 7:11). Here are two forces at work which have not been employed since. This is what Peter refers to when he says that certain events have occurred in the past, in the natural realm, which are not reflected in present day activity (2 Pet. 3:5–7). First, the fountains of the deep burst forth. That seems to suggest that the level of the oceans was raised. Possibly the floors of the oceans were raised up so that the sea inundated the earth with great tidal waves.

Second, the windows of heaven were opened and the rain poured out—not merely for a few hours, as we see in our day, but for forty days and forty nights. Here is far more rainfall than can be accounted for by the normal process of evaporation and precipitation. From somewhere there came vast quantities of water upon the earth, both from above and from below. This has given rise to several interesting theories about the flood. There is, for instance, the "canopy" theory—the idea that the earth at one time was very much like the planet Saturn, surrounded by rings which forced a canopy over the earth. Many astronomers believe that the rings of Saturn are made up of ice particles, which would, of course, be water suspended in vast, thick rings around the planet. If something like that were true of the earth of that day, then perhaps the flood represents a collapse of a similar canopy of vapor or ice.

This may account for what has been a puzzle to scientists for generations: the sudden death of large numbers of great mammoths and other animals which are found imbedded in ice. They have been discovered by the thousands, and some estimate even millions, in the Arctic regions. Evidently at one time the area was tropical, but it was suddenly plunged into sub-freezing temperatures of such intensity that animals immediately perished, frozen in a quick deep-freeze that preserved them through the centuries since. They are discovered with bits of grass still in their mouths, unchewed—so sudden was their death.

Another theory says that all these events were brought about by the near approach to earth of a heavenly body. A few years ago scientists were watching the approach to earth of one of the asteroids, a miniature planet called "Icarus," which was nearing the earth at a great speed. There was a time when scientists were saying that if Icarus had deviated less than one percent from its course, it would have swung into a collision with the earth. There is a possibility that a near approach of a planetary body to the earth in Noah's day upset the whole gravitational equilibrium of the earth, raised the ocean levels, created tides both of water and possibly of the solid earth itself, and thus caused the flood. Now I must hasten to point out that all such scientific guesses are but theories. The Bible does not teach these, but simply implies that something like these may be indicated.

Verse 16 of this passage adds another significant thought: "And they that entered, male and female of all flesh, went in as God had commanded him; and the Lord shut him in." Noah did not slam the door shut; God shut it. He shut it seven days before the first raindrop fell. While the sun was yet shining and the sky was blue, while the people around were still convinced that nothing was going to happen, God shut Noah in so that he could not get out. You can see how this pictures beautifully what Paul calls "the sealing of the Spirit," in the Epistle to the Ephesians. Those who enter our ark, the Lord Jesus Christ, are sealed by God, kept by the power of God, safe in Christ.

Sudden Destruction

The third emphasis of this passage is given in these last verses:

> The flood continued forty days upon the earth; and the waters increased, and bore up the ark, and it rose high above the earth. The waters prevailed and increased greatly upon the earth; and the ark floated on the face of the waters. And the waters prevailed so mightily upon the earth that all the high mountains under the whole heaven were covered; the waters prevailed above the mountains, covering them fifteen cubits deep. And all flesh died that moved upon the earth, birds, cattle, beasts, all swarming creatures that swarm upon the earth [insects], and every man; everything on the dry land in whose nostrils was the breath of life died. He blotted out every living thing that was upon the face of the ground, man and animals and creeping things and birds of the air; they were blotted out from the earth. Only Noah was left, and those that were with him in the ark. And the waters prevailed upon the earth a hundred and fifty days (Gen. 7:17–24).

What a striking thing, the extent of the judgment of the flood! Many have raised the question, was the flood universal—did it cover the entire earth? It is very difficult to answer that. We have a suggestion in the next chapter, which I have already commented on, that the nature of the flood was to produce vast tidal waves which swept across the earth. Perhaps this may account for the fact that the mountains were covered (occasionally, at least) to a depth of fifteen cubits when these gigantic waves swept in. I think it is necessary to point out that when it speaks of "the whole earth," the Hebrew word can also be translated "the whole land." This is what has made many wonder if perhaps the flood was more or less localized. Certainly it was wide in extent, perhaps covering a quarter or half of the earth, but possibly not all of it. Certainly, there is no theological necessity for a universal flood. What is taught in the Scriptures is that we are all united together as descendants of Adam. So, theologically, there is perhaps some reason to view this as a limited flood.

But one thing is certainly clear. The flood destroyed the civilization of that day. "The world that then was," says the Apostle Peter, "perished." The civilization of that day came to an abrupt and sudden end. The Scripture warns throughout of the suddenness of God's judgment. Every day bears testimony to the suddenness with which death can strike in individual lives. This was underscored for me one time when I had a near-fatal accident. Driving down the highway north of Davis, California, I was about ready to enter the freeway at highway 80, when a man in a blue pickup truck, waiting by the side of the road, suddenly pulled into my path. My immediate thought was, "Well, this is it. I'll not get through this," for it looked impossible. But by God's grace I was able to swerve around him to the front, and he stopped enough that I was able to get by him. Had he not stopped he would have rolled me over, but as it was, only the rear end of my car was damaged. None of us was hurt and we were both able to drive on after the accident. But it was a very close shave; I didn't have time to pray, just to act.

That sort of thing, the Bible says, can happen to an age as well. That is the whole meaning of this passage. The fabric of our society can grow so rotten it can no longer support itself. Like a sail in a tempest, a tear appears which rapidly rips open and soon the whole thing is in tatters. A total collapse follows once the process begins. That is the lesson of the flood. It is clear from this and every account in Scripture that the great and fateful questions of faith are addressed to us privately and almost inaudibly. Seldom does God confront us with dramatic moments of decision. These people before the flood surely would have wished that the thunder would have rolled a week ahead. That would have tipped them off. But the skies were clear, and Noah was shut into the ark, while there was no physical sign of impending judgment. The people were shut up to believing or disbelieving the offer that God made them through Noah.

Is not that the lesson of our day? Remember how Jesus said that no one would return from the dead to witness to the five brothers of the man who was in hell? (Luke 16:27 ff). No, that will not happen. "They have Moses and the prophets, let them hear them." Thus we are right now facing the decisive events of our lives, in this word from God. We do not have to wait until after our second heart attack; we must make a decision now on the basis of what is set before us now. We cannot presume to wait until some tremendous catastrophe occurs. A lady handed me a note from her son the other day in which he said, "When I see the world burning, in fulfillment of the prophecies, then I'll believe." That is too late. That is also what these people said. When we hear the rain coming and the thunder rolling, we'll believe. But God had shut the door, and it was too late.

Do you take that seriously? You may die tomorrow, who knows? The great question of Scripture is, if life is that uncertain, why not live now? Not in the empty death of the world's delirium, but in the full swing of the Spirit's power, knowing that all that is truly vital is kept in the ark of Jesus Christ; "kept by the power of God, unto salvation yet to be revealed in the last time," says the

Apostle Peter. Whatever comes upon the earth, the word of the Lord Jesus to us is, "When you see these things begin to come to pass, lift up your head and rejoice." Why? Because you know that what destroys others is, in the wisdom of God, compelled to bear you up, as Noah and the ark were born up by the waters that destroyed the earth. That is why Jesus says, "Look up, lift up your head, and rejoice." If your relationship to God is right, the very things that destroy others and tear them apart will but add to your faith, bear you up, and keep you safe whatever that tribulation or testing may be.

Will you sit in quietness for a moment, with your own thoughts before the Lord? Does it frighten you to remain quiet before God? Do you know him well enough to welcome it? Do you get restless, nervous, eager to be away? This One who is the most important Being in the world, with whom you must reckon—are you afraid of him? If so, that should tell you volumes about yourself. Where are you in respect to the ark which moves through the deluge of our present generation? Are you in it—or outside it? Do you know Jesus Christ, really know him, so that you demonstrate it in your life? Or are you outside, perishing, drowning?

> *Our father, what a wonderful faculty your Word has of stripping off veils, removing illusions, taking away deceit from our eyes. Let us look at life as it is—how dark it is in many ways and yet how light, when viewed in relationship to the Lord Jesus Christ, to whom all power is given in heaven and on earth. Thank you, Lord, for the hope that is set before us, for the promises that undergird us, for the love that surrounds us and calls us by his power in this day and age. Amen.*

8

The New Beginning

Now WE EMERGE from the ark with Noah into a new world and a new beginning. We have already seen that though these stories in the Old Testament are actual history—that is, they are not myth but actual historic occurrences—they are also prototypes of the spiritual history each of us can experience. In other words, we reproduce these stories in the course of our spiritual pilgrimage. Since this is so, then every detail of these stories is highly significant to us. The Old Testament is deliberately designed to illustrate to us what is going on in our own lives.

The flood, as we have already seen, is not only a picture of judgment, but also of a new creation, a new beginning —and for us, a new birth. Paul describes the new birth in 2 Corinthians: "Therefore, if any one is in Christ, he is a new creation; the old has passed away, behold, the new has come" (2 Cor. 5:17). But the flood is also a picture of smaller events of our lives which involve a crisis of judgment and a new beginning. Such events occur all the time in Christian experience. This reduplication is the way nature functions also. We know that the smallest atom is built along the general pattern of the whole solar system. In the atom, God reproduces in miniature what he writes large across the great wheeling canvas of space. So these stories of the Old Testament reproduce both the great crisis experiences of our spiritual pilgrimage, and the miniature crises as well. Every experience of forgiveness is like a mini-flood wherein we miraculously survive a potential spiritual disaster and are brought safely through to repentance and cleansing. If you have experienced that, you have also shared in some degree Noah's experience in the flood.

Throughout chapter 8 of Genesis we will note the alternation of the activity of God and Noah. God acts first to create a certain situation, then Noah reacts to that situation. This is the way it is in the Christian life as well. As always, the initiative is taken by God.

But God remembered Noah and all the beasts and all the cattle that were with him in the ark. And God made a wind blow over the earth, and the waters subsided; the fountains of the deep and the windows of the heavens were closed, the rain from the heavens was restrained, and the waters receded from the earth continually. At the end of a hundred and fifty days the waters had abated; and in the seventh month, on the seventeenth day of the month, the ark came to rest upon the mountains of Ararat. And the waters continued to abate until the tenth month; in the tenth month, on the first day of the month, the tops of the mountains were seen (Gen. 8:1–5).

We are told that "God remembered Noah." Wherever Scripture uses the phrase, "God remembered," it marks the activity of God on behalf of those whom he so remembers. God remembered Noah and all the beasts and all the cattle that were with him in the ark. This is a charming way of saying that God thought constantly about them. He was concerned about Noah and the dumb beasts that were with him. I think we can justifiably extend this to see a picture of God's concern also for the church and the world. Noah represents the people of God in any age—the church in our age—and, though this is not very complimentary, the dumb beasts in the ark represent worldlings. The unregenerate, in their blindness and their incapacity to help themselves, are frequently compared in Scripture to dumb, irrational beasts. These characteristics are manifested in history in the constant blunders made by a secular society, and by the impossible problems that arise out of secular thinking. This is often called to our attention today when the thinkers, the philosophers, the statesmen of our age, are confessing with embarrassing frequency their bewilderment and bafflement at the problems they are facing and their utter incapacity to solve them.

For Noah's Sake

But God saves the world for the sake of his people. He preserved the animals in the ark for Noah's sake. He "remembered" them for Noah's sake. The Word of God alone gives us the true picture of the structure of society. God deals with the secular world on the basis of, and for the sake of, his people. What his people are will determine what God does with the world. This is what Jesus meant when he said, "You are the salt of the earth, you are the light of the world." Far too little has been said about this from the pulpit. The business of preaching is to help Christians see that they are responsible for the way society goes. We must learn this, for history and Scripture both unite to confirm it.

So God moves to save the beasts and cattle because of Noah. The result is, the wind blows upon the earth. Throughout Scripture, the wind is a picture and symbol of the Holy Spirit in his sovereign activity. Jesus said to Nicodemus, "The wind blows where it wishes, and you hear the sound thereof, but you cannot direct its activity." You cannot predict where the wind is going to blow; it is sovereign. And you cannot understand it; it is mysterious. It is amazing that even in this day of advanced meteorology we still do not understand much about the blowing of the wind. It is an apt symbol of the Holy Spirit whose sovereign activity is essential to mankind.

As the wind blew, the account tells us, the strange forces which produced the flood were reversed. The fountains of the deep and the windows of the heavens were closed. Thus, these two unique forces, which have never been active on earth since that time, were reversed and the waters began to subside. The waters apparently flowed back into the ocean basins, the floor of the ocean subsiding to its present level, and the hills and mountains changing, rising and falling in various places. This perhaps explains the great boneyards—especially upon hilltops—where great numbers of bones of animals and birds are found mingled together. These may well be the direct result of the flood. As the account tells us, the water receded, and in the Hebrew it is made clear they receded in tides, "going and coming," which is translated in our version "continually." It indicates great tides washing around the earth.

Sign of a New World

What is particularly significant in this section is the date on which the ark grounded on the hills of Ararat, which is given very precisely. It was the first sign to Noah and the inhabitants of the ark that a new world was about to appear from the waters. Their first ground of confidence that the judgment was abating and the flood waters were receding was when they felt the ark ground itself upon the mountains of Ararat. The date, you may be amazed to learn, is the exact day of the year when, centuries later, Jesus rose from the dead.

In Exodus, chapter 12, we are told that at the giving of the Passover God changed the seventh month to the first month. He made Passover the beginning of the year, though previously the beginning of the year had come in the fall. On the fourteenth day of the first month (which was formerly the seventh month) the Passover was to be eaten. We know from the Gospels that on the day the Passover was eaten our Lord died in Jerusalem. Three days from the fourteenth would bring us to the seventeenth, and on the seventeenth day of the first month Jesus rose from the dead. That would be the same as the seventh day of the seventh month in the old reckoning of this passage in Genesis. It is most significant that the ark grounded upon the mountains of Ararat on the same calendar day on which our Lord rose from the dead, thus signifying that life in the new earth for God's people was to rest upon resurrection power. I do not think you could possibly have a clearer picture than this portrayal of the basis for our life in this present world.

Now Noah is expected to act upon God's activity. So the Christian life is not to be a passive, lazy experience but a continual response to God's activity. We read in the next section,

> At the end of forty days Noah opened the window of the ark which he had made, and sent forth a raven; and it went to and fro until the waters were dried up from the earth. Then he sent forth a dove from him, to see if the waters had subsided from the face of the ground; but the dove found no place to set her foot, and she returned to him to the ark, for the waters were still on the face of the whole earth. So he put forth his hand and took her and brought her into the ark with him. He waited another seven days, and again he sent forth the dove out of the ark; and the dove came back to him in the evening, and lo, in her mouth a freshly plucked olive leaf; so Noah knew that the waters had subsided from the earth. Then he waited another seven days, and sent forth the dove; and she did not return to him any more (Gen. 8:6–12).

What shall we make of this strange story of the raven and the dove? They are clearly symbolical, even though also historical. The raven is listed in Leviticus as one of the unclean birds, forbidden to the Jewish people to eat. It is the first bird that is released from the ark. According to the Hebrew, it flew to and fro, never returning to the ark, evidently feeding upon carrion and resting upon floating carcasses that were there in abundance during the flood. As the account makes clear, the raven is no help to Noah whatsoever. The release of the raven tells him nothing about the condition of earth. Noah sees it flying to and fro above the waters, seemingly quite satisfied with the conditions it finds. It does not return to the ark but rests upon floating carcasses and feeds upon them. The dove, on the other hand, is a clean bird. It does not fly abroad and remain, but returns to the ark. It rests only in the

ark until a new world is ready for it. On its last return it
brings an olive leaf in its bill as a symbol of life and peace.

Conflicting Natures

Now what does this all mean? It clearly pictures facts
to which we must relate daily. In our present life, according to the Scriptures, though we are redeemed, there are
two natures present within us. One is truly ours; the other
is an imposter which is no longer ours, as Paul puts it in
Romans 7, but with which we must contend until we are
released from its presence by the resurrection of the body.
One is called "the flesh" and the other "the spirit." The
whole struggle of the spiritual life arises out of the con-
flict of the flesh with the spirit, and the spirit against the
flesh. One is evil, unclean; the other is clean and good.
These are symbolized by these two birds. It is God's way
of telling us that in the present age, like Noah, we must
live with two natures: one which is truly ours, and one
which is an imposter.

One is like a raven: it rests and feeds on anything. It
finds delight even in carrion, in foul and filthy things.
But it is of no help to us. If we rely on it, we will learn
nothing worthwhile about ourselves or the world around
us. It is useless as far as any profit in life is concerned.
That is the flesh. Scripture is utterly consistent in these
things, teaching us all the way through of the worthless-
ness and emptiness of the flesh in its apparent ability to
think, reason, and act. It is all worthless, and God pro-
nounces it so in the cross. That is the offense of the cross.
The natural man does not like to be told that all that he
can do apart from God is useless, yet that is exactly what
the Lord Jesus says. He told his disciples, "without me,
you can do nothing." It is not that they would not be

active, but there would be nothing worthwhile, nothing of any value, nothing that would enhance or bless or strengthen or prove at last to be gold, silver, or precious stones. It would all be wood, hay, and stubble; an imposing facade with nothing behind it.

At a baccalaureate service held at Stanford Memorial Church in which I took part some years ago, there was a strange mixture of truth and error. The music was great, consisting of great hymns of the church, but much of what was said was directly contrary to the Christian position. I kept a copy of the responsive reading which was used in place of Scripture. It reads, in part:

> The whole nature of man must be used wisely by the one who desires to enter the way. Each man is to himself absolutely the way, the truth, and the life. Seek it by plunging into the mysterious and glorious depths of your own inmost being.

There is the raven flying. It is so much humanistic gas! No wonder our present generation looks in vain to the secular wisdom of the world to guide it. How can it guide when it feeds on that kind of carrion?

In contrast to that is the dove, our true nature which can only find rest in the ark, in Jesus Christ, until a new world is made ready for it. This is exactly the experience we are going through now, is it not? We have a new nature within, a nature imparted by Jesus Christ; his life joined with our life, his Spirit bearing witness with our spirit that we are the children of God, born again, waiting in the ark for a new world to arise. That new spirit bears witness within of life and peace in Jesus Christ. It brings to us the olive leaf. This is truth we need to know to cope with the world in which we live, just as this was expressive of truth Noah needed to know to live in the world of his day.

Now we come to Noah's emergence from the ark:

> In the six hundred and first year, in the first month, the first day of the month, the waters were dried from off the earth; and Noah removed the covering of the ark, and looked, and behold, the face of the ground was dry. In the second month, on the twenty-seventh day of the month, the earth was dry. Then God said to Noah, "Go forth from the ark, you and your wife, and your sons and your sons' wives with you. Bring forth with you every living thing that is with you of all flesh—birds and animals and every creeping thing that creeps on the earth—that they may breed abundantly on the earth, and be fruitful and multiply upon the earth." So Noah went forth, and his sons and his wife and his sons' wives with him. And every beast, every creeping thing, and every bird, everything that moves upon the earth, went forth by families out of the ark (Gen. 8:13–19).

Again, the date of this act of Noah's is significant. We are told it was the six hundred and first year (of Noah's life), in the first month, the first day of the month. In the Scriptures, the number six is the number of man. Noah spent his six hundredth year in the ark, as symbolic of what man alone produces—nothing but a hiding from judgment. But at the very beginning of the seventh century of his life (seven is the number of perfection), the first year, the first month, and the first day, he left the ark to go out into a new world, a new beginning. This is symbolic of the beginning of a Christian life. It marks the end of the old, the end of our dependence on ourselves, and the beginning of our dependence on God. It is to be lived in a world which is yet a mixture of good and evil, truth and error, but it is a new beginning. "If any man be in Christ, he is a new creation; old things have passed away, behold, all things become new."

The next step is God's; he commands, "Go forth from the ark." It is striking throughout this whole story the way God directs the activity of Noah. He is the one who says, "Make an ark for the saving of yourself and the animal world." He is also the one who says, "Come into the ark." Now he is the one who says, "Go forth from the ark." The timing is God's, and the initiative is God's. For Noah there is nothing but simple acts of obedience. Safely, securely, through all the difficulties and problems, God's word leads him to do the right action at the right time. Isn't this exactly what we are called to? We make the ark, like Noah, when we learn of Jesus Christ. We are commanded to learn of him. When we expose ourselves to the Christian message, we learn of Christ, and thus make an ark for ourselves. We come into the ark when we trust the grace of our Lord Jesus, when we trust his word, believe him, and rest upon what he said. Then we go forth from the ark when we act as redeemed men and women in a lost world—when we act as forgiven sinners, living by the grace and constant presence of God in our lives, in the midst of an ungodly generation.

A Sweet Savor

It is fitting, therefore, that the chapter should close with a scene of thanksgiving and of promise.

> Then Noah built an altar to the Lord, and took of every clean animal and of every clean bird, and offered burnt offerings on the altar. And when the Lord smelled the pleasing odor, the Lord said in his heart, "I will never again curse the ground because of man, for the imagination of man's heart is evil from his youth; neither will I

ever again destroy every living creature as I have done. While the earth remains, seedtime and harvest, cold and heat, summer and winter, day and night, shall not cease" (Gen. 8:20–22).

The striking thing is that the *first* thing Noah does when he leaves the ark is to give thanks to God. Wouldn't you think he would at least have stopped to cook a meal? No, this man knows how to put first things first. The first thing he does is to give thanks to God. What a scene, as they knelt down in the mud and gave thanks. It is the constant call of God to man, "Give thanks, give thanks." How many times do you read in the Scriptures, especially in the Epistles, that Christians are to rejoice. "Give thanks, for this is the will of God in Christ Jesus concerning you." Giving thanks means to recognize reality. When you give thanks, you are recognizing the undergirding of God, the presence of God in the midst of life, and his control over the affairs of life. Thus, you cannot give thanks without recognizing the situation as it really is. In Romans 1, God's charge to a false and godless world is that "although they knew God they did not honor him as God or give thanks to him." They did not recognize the basis upon which their life was built. Though they would not hesitate to thank someone who so much as picked up a handkerchief for them, they could find no time to stop and give thanks to the God upon whom their life depended. But Noah built an altar and he gave thanks to God for his deliverance.

God said, "Never again will I send a flood upon the earth, *because* the imagination of man's heart is evil from his youth." There's nothing that a flood can do to change the heart. Destruction does not change it, so God does not send a flood again. Another means must be found to change man. Thus God lays the groundwork for a fresh proclamation of the message of redemption to a new world. We read that Noah's thanksgiving was a sweet savor in the nostrils of God. This does not mean that God smelled a barbecue over the fence, as you do sometimes, and his mouth began to water. Some of the old Babylonian accounts which parallel the flood story say that the gods had grown ravenous because of the lack of men's offering during the days of the flood, and when Noah offered his sacrifice, the gods gathered like vultures above it. That, of course, is myth, but it does catch one great note of truth: that God delights in man's thanksgiving and praise. It is a sweet savor to him of Jesus Christ.

That is the point of this account. God saw, in this act of Noah, the total givingness of Jesus, the fact that here was One who, like these sacrifices, yielded up his life for the sake of what would be accomplished thereby, without reluctance, but gladly, willingly. As God saw that reflected in Noah's sacrifice, it was to him the fragrance of Christ. That is what God is after in our lives. How do you glorify God? How do you live for his honor? By giving yourself, that's the way. That is what true love does.

The world is constantly talking to us today about rights. "Claim your rights, demand your rights, stand for your rights." That is exactly the opposite of the Spirit of Jesus Christ. "If you lose your life, you will save it," he said. If in selfishness and greed you demand your life and try to hang on to it, you will lose it. God has written that across the pages of history, and he writes that across the page of every individual life. "He that saves his life shall lose it, but he that loses his life for my sake shall find it." To "lose" your life is a sweet savor of Jesus Christ.

God's response is to give man a promise. We read, "While the earth remains, seedtime and harvest, cold and heat, summer and winter, day and night, shall not cease." The revolution of the earth around the sun, its rotation upon its axis, will never stop again. The laws of nature will remain steady and dependable. If man plants seed, there will come a harvest later. It all rests on the faithfulness of God. God's Word declares this and thousands of years of human history testify to the truth of this verse. Never again has God allowed these things to cease. This verse implies that part of what caused the flood was some hesitation in the revolution of the earth, or in its rotation. But never again, God says, shall that happen, because that does not change the nature of man. World catastrophe will not change man. There is only one thing that changes man: the grace of a living God revealed in Jesus Christ. "I am the way, the truth, and the life," says Jesus. "No man comes to the Father but by me."

We are sobered, Father, as we think how our very lives depend upon your faithful word; how the existence of this planet, its place in the galaxy, its revolution around the sun, its rotation around its axis, the production of flowers and grain and food and fruit, all rest upon a faithful God. We praise you, Lord, that our redemption, our deliverance from the sin that eats away at the vitals of humanity, also rests upon that same faithful word. We pray that there may be a sweet savor of Christ going up to you as you sense a willingness of men and women to give themselves—husbands, to give themselves to their wives; wives, to give themselves to their husbands; parents, to give themselves to their children; children, to give themselves to their parents; friends, to give themselves to each other; men and women to give themselves for their enemies; to love, to honor, and to obey your word. We ask it in Jesus' name, Amen.

9

Rules of the Game

THE NINTH CHAPTER OF GENESIS records one of the major covenants of the Bible, a covenant God made with Noah immediately following the flood, but beyond Noah, with all humanity. This covenant is the basis for all human government today. It contains God's provision for the ordering of human life. These provisions are intended to govern life in the world following the flood. As the Apostle Peter makes clear in the New Testament, we live in that same world. It will continue until the great day when fire judges the present world.

These biblical covenants are not agreements with God hammered out at a bargaining table. God is never forced to come to terms with the rebellion of man. He is always in control of history; he always has been and always will be. Man is never a threat to the government of God. We must learn to understand that or we will never have any comprehension of the course of history. Therefore, these covenants must never be thought of as bargains that man makes with God. These are, rather, rules of the game under which all humanity must live. We do not have any options. It is God who determines them, and man obeys them whether he likes it or not. It is impossible to break the laws of God; you can only illustrate them. If you jump from a 30-story building you will not break the law of gravity; you will only illustrate it. (That is what's called jumping to a conclusion.)

Now here the covenant is made not only with Noah, but as verse 17 of chapter 9 indicates, it is made with "all flesh that is upon the earth." Therefore, it is a covenant that governs human life, wherever and whenever it is found. Let us look at the eight specific provisions which God put into force with the whole earth at the time following the flood. They have been in effect since that day, and no man can evade them.

This covenant actually begins in Genesis 6 where we have the first mention of it in verse 18. The first provision of the covenant is God's intent to preserve mankind, through Noah. This has already been fulfilled, as we have seen.

> "But I will establish my covenant with you; and you shall come into the ark, you, your sons, your wife, and your sons' wives with you."

Thus mankind was preserved through the flood. That is the first thing in the agreement God made with Noah.

The second feature is found in the closing verses of chapter 8, which we have also looked at briefly. This second provision establishes the dependability of nature:

> And when the Lord smelled the pleasing odor, the Lord
> said in his heart, "I will never again curse the ground
> because of man, for the imagination of man's heart is
> evil from his youth; neither will I ever again destroy
> every living creature as I have done. While the earth
> remains, seedtime and harvest, cold and heat, summer
> and winter, day and night, shall not cease" (Gen. 8:21–
> 22).

Today we look back upon thousands of years which
testify to the faithfulness of that promise. God has made
nature utterly dependable. This predictability is the basis
of all modern science and investigation. God has created
a nature that is dependable and upon which men can
rely. The only mistake scientists make is that they rule out
the possibility of divine intervention and that, the Bible
makes clear, is always God's reserved right. He can intervene in his own scheme any time he chooses, and has
done so in the past.

The Reason for Covenants

Also in these verses we learn the fundamental reason
God makes covenants with men. It is given in verse 21.
"Because," God says, "the imagination of man's heart is
evil from his youth." That is the fundamental truth which
God is forever seeking to impress upon men. Man, who
was made in the image of God and to share the glory of
God, has become distorted and twisted by the invasion of
an evil principle which enslaves the mind, will, and emo-
tions of men. Therefore, fallen man is a victim of evil
imaginations from his youth on. That is the basis for the
wonderful fact that the Bible declares about humanity,
but also the basis for the wonderful story of God's love
and redemption. If this declaration is not true, then the

story of Jesus Christ is not true, and the need for God's redeeming grace is denied.

It is for this reason God labors to impress this fact upon men. It is the fundamental fact we must learn. In order to teach it, God establishes human life in such a way as to make men face up to this overwhelming fact. It is the one fact above all others which man most strongly resists. Read the analyses of the world's thinkers, and everywhere you see how they cling to the big lie that man at heart is decent and good and loving. Thus, every panacea man proposes is unworkable to start with because it is based on a false conception of humanity. You can see this in the Letters to the Editor column in any newspaper. There proposals made for the solution of the problems of mankind invariably are based upon the idea that man is basically good. Just give him a chance and all that is within will work out to the benefit of all. The difficulty of changing man's mind on this is reflected by these words of Philip Mauro, a very astute Christian lawyer.

Among the strong delusions of these times there is none stronger than that Man's Day is a day of glorious achievement, successive triumphs, and continuous progress, and that by the forces operating in it, mankind is eventually to be brought to a condition of universal blessedness and contentment.

The writer knows full well that those who are under the influence of this delusion cannot be freed from it by arguments, however cogent, or by statistics showing the appalling increase of crime, accidents, suicides, and insanity, or by the open and flagrant manifestations of corruption, lawlessness, and profligacy. To all these appeals they resolutely close their eyes and ears, not willing to recognize the real drift and the certain end of what is called civilization.

That is well put. In order to impress this truth upon the reluctant heart of man, God orders human life in such a way that we cannot escape exposure to this fundamental revelation of the heart of fallen man, "the imagination of man's heart is evil from his youth." Every provision of this covenant made with Noah and the whole human race is designed to impress upon man the helplessness of his evil condition, and thus to drive him to the love and grace of God. Only God can save man. That is the whole point of history. God begins by making nature stable and dependable, so that man cannot blame his evil on the capriciousness of nature. We will note as we go through how each feature of the covenant stresses and underscores this fact of human evil.

The third provision, found in chapter 9, verses 1 and 2, is to disclose man's rule over the animal world through fear:

> And God blessed Noah and his sons, and said to them, "Be fruitful and multiply, and fill the earth. The fear of you and the dread of you shall be upon every beast of the earth, and upon every bird of the air, upon everything that creeps on the ground and all the fish of the sea; into your hand they are delivered" (Gen. 9:1–2).

Why do animals fear man? Oh, I know this fear can be overcome by patient training, but there is an instinctive dread and fear of man in the animal creation, and there are some animals which man has never been able to tame. Why? Well, it is all designed to teach us that man is not what he once was. He is no longer lord of creation, with the animal world in loving, obedient subjection to him. Now he finds the animals fearing him, hiding from him, and running from him. It is the way God has of reminding us that the image of God in man is twisted and distorted, and love has been replaced by fear.

Borrowed Life Force

Now the fourth provision of the covenant is to provide a life that comes out of death.

"Every moving thing that lives shall be food for you; and as I gave you the green plants, I now give you everything" (Gen. 9:3).

Animal life is now made the proper food of man. It is all designed that every meal should remind us that life is made possible only by the death of another creature. We are alive only because other creatures have died on our behalf to sustain our life. If not animals, then plants, at least. We do not live in and of ourselves, we live by feeding upon other life. Now this ought to impress upon us a fundamental fact of life, that we are not independent creatures, going our own way, master of our own fate. We are the most dependent of creatures. We have no life force of our own; it is all borrowed. That is why Jesus said, in fulfillment of the truth toward which all this points, "Unless you eat the flesh of the Son of Man and drink his blood, you have no life in you; he who eats my flesh and drinks my blood has eternal life" (Jn. 6:53–54). He did not mean that literally, but symbolically, spiritually. We are to feed on him, and draw from him all that we need. He is designed for life, and without Jesus Christ we can never fulfill the humanity that throbs in each one's being.

The fifth provision of this covenant teaches the sacredness of human life:

Only you shall not eat flesh with its life, that is, its blood. For your lifeblood I will surely require a reckoning; of every beast I will require it and of man; of every man's brother I will require the life of man. Whoever sheds the blood of man, by man shall his blood be shed; for God made man in his own image" (Gen. 9:4–6).

There is tremendous significance in this passage. Here we are told that man may eat the flesh of animals, but not the blood. Why? Because, says God, the life is in the blood, and life is God's property. It is never man's property. Man does not impart life; he does not originate it, and it does not belong to him. Therefore, he has no right to take life. That is what this teaches. Life is God's property. Even in the proper taking of animal life (which is permitted man), he still must recognize the sovereignty and authority of God over life. Therefore, says God, do not eat the blood, because the blood is the life of the animal.

Man is not an absolute monarch, as he so fondly imagines, but he must live his life under God, in relationship to God. There are things which God says are off limits for him. This is particularly true of the life of man. The text goes on to tell us, "For *your* lifeblood I will surely require a reckoning." The life of man is peculiarly sacred to God; only God has the right to take it. If anyone else violates this, God says he will require a reckoning, and it is a terrible price that God extracts. We will see what it is shortly. It is *always* paid. There is never escape from this. God says, "I will *surely* require a reckoning."

Now it is not merely retribution, it is not the taking of vengeance upon another for the murder of a man. Some have read this Scripture as though it justified blood vengeance, and terrible feuds have erupted and run on for centuries in which one murder is avenged by another, and that by still another, until whole families are ravaged. But God, all through the Scriptures, reserves vengeance unto himself. Remember how Paul puts it, quoting the Old Testament: "Vengeance is mine, I will repay, says the Lord" (Rom. 12:19). You have no right to take vengeance into your own hands, says God. It is my task. You don't know what will happen, and you can't control the evil effects. Leave it up to me; vengeance is mine, I will repay.

But I do think there is justification for taking this verse as a basis for capital punishment. "Whoever sheds the blood of man, by man shall his blood be shed" is the instruction God gives to government for the taking of life under certain conditions. As the Apostle Paul makes clear, government acts as the instrument of God. It is the agent of God. In Romans 13 government is seen as the servant of God in this sense, and it "does not bear the sword in vain" (Rom. 13:4). It is thus God who takes human life when it is done through proper governmental channels, and therefore it is not murder, as many are calling it today.

Furthermore, it is clear from this passage that capital punishment is not necessarily intended to be a deterrent to crime. There is much we ought to learn from this by studying it through carefully. I am sure that capital punishment *is* a deterrent to crime—despite many published articles which attempt to prove the reverse—but it is not intended to be that alone. If so, why would God require, as this passage makes clear, the death of an animal who killed a man? Later on, under the law, if an animal accidentally or deliberately killed a man, the animal's life was forfeit. God required that the animal be slain, as he says also here, "Of every beast I will require it." What is the point of that? Surely not to deter crime among the animals. No, the purpose for this is to teach us that human life is off limits. Only God has the right to take it. It is to be taken only under the conditions which he prescribes. If even an animal touches a man, he must be slain to impress upon us that God highly values individual human life. Could anything be clearer than this?

We can hear in this the echoes of God's words to Cain after the murder of his brother, Abel, "The voice of your brother's blood is crying to me from the ground." Murder makes a claim upon God, upon his justice and his power. Injustice, violence, and bloodshed all cry out to the justice of God for correction, and God cannot ignore it. Remember that God set a mark on Cain to teach men that they must not take vengeance into their own hands, that even an outright acknowledged murderer is not to be prey to any other human who desires vengeance. But man before the flood, in his evil, twisted that restriction to his own advantage and used it to justify violence (as you see in the case of Lamech, in chapter 4). The result was the spreading of violence throughout the earth which resulted at last in the judgment of the flood. The earth was filled with violence in those days.

Brothers in Adam

Now, after the flood, God is reinstating this prohibition against taking human life, but he controls it by another tactic. He says he will extract a price for any blood that is shed: "Whoever sheds the blood of man, by man shall his blood be shed; for God made man in his own image."

Now, that is more than the process of justice. Human justice does not always do the job; it sometimes fails. But notice what God says just before this: "Of every man's brother I will require the life of man." God does not look at humanity as we do. We look around and see so many isolated individuals. We say we live our own lives; we have our own programs. We think of ourselves as separate from one another. But God never does. He looks at us and sees the ties that bind us together—the ties that unite us to the past, and to the past beyond that. In God's sight, the human race is one vast body of humanity, a brotherhood—a brotherhood of one flesh "in Adam." God says that he will require of this entire race a price for the shed blood of a single individual. Murder will be avenged against the race, not merely against the guilty individual. A price is extracted from the whole vast race of mankind.

Now we are touching upon a principle that has always been active in history: violence begets violence. God has ordained it so. The man's evil looms so large that people cease their delusive, naive ideas and recognize the stark, naked fact of human evil and turn to the God who alone can deal with the problems. Since man is a brotherhood, it means that the innocent can suffer as well as the guilty. The innocent individual will be struck down as well as the guilty because we are all tied together and the blood price is extracted against the race. In the memorial service for his brother, Ted Kennedy quoted something Bob Kennedy had said that reflected this very concept of the brotherhood of man, the brotherhood in Adam. (That is different than the brotherhood in Christ.) This is what Robert F. Kennedy said:

> But we can perhaps remember—if only for a time—that those who live with us are our brothers, that they share with us the same short moment of life; that they seek—as we do—nothing but the chance to live out their lives in purpose and happiness, winning what satisfaction and fulfillment they can.
> Surely this bond of common faith, this bond of common goal, can begin to teach us something. Surely we

can learn, at least, to look at those around us as fellow men. And surely we can begin to work a little harder to bind up the wounds among us and to become in our own hearts brothers and countrymen once again.

That is exactly what God wants to teach us. When men resort to violence to gain their ends in one area, they may justify it as being peculiarly needed to accomplish their specific goal, but what they don't see is that, though God apparently does nothing to correct it in that one area, soon a war breaks out or the accident rate increases or a senseless murder occurs or violence sweeps a city or a public figure is assassinated. Men are then forced to learn that God does not take lightly the distorting and despoiling of his image in man. He says he will not, and he never has. That is why violence inevitably breeds more violence, until man at last, in horror at what he has loosed in society, faces up to the fundamental fact that he is infiltrated with evil. Only God can cure it. Only the cross of Jesus Christ can smash this evil in any one of us. That is what God wants us to learn.

Now the sixth provision of this covenant is to instill a desire to multiply and populate the earth: "And you, be fruitful and multiply, bring forth abundantly on the earth and multiply in it" (Gen. 9:7). In the light of what we have just seen that seems a strange thing for God to say. Recognizing, as he does, since he is a God of realism, that man is the slave of an evil principle within him, why should he want the earth to be filled with this? Why should he command that the earth be populated by means of human reproduction? The answer is that in isolation man finds it easy to maintain the illusion of his basic decency and his independence from God.

I was raised in Montana where we had a very low population density. I knew certain aloof individuals, recluses, who lived out in the hills by themselves—perhaps half a dozen of them—but I never knew one who didn't feel that he was a very good, lovable, and kind individual, though the rest of the community did not share that opinion. In isolation we do not have to look at ourselves. But as the world fills up and we can no longer move away from those that irritate us, we are forced to face our own sinfulness. As the cities increase in population, the earth fills up, the continents overflow, and there is no place to run, men discover what has always been true: that under crowded conditions the thin veneer of culture disappears fast and all that is hidden underneath breaks out. Winston Churchill once commented on the fact that men labor under the delusion that man is basically decent and good. But, he said, given sufficient stress, put under the proper pressure, "Modern man will do anything, and his modern woman will back him up."

The seventh provision of the covenant is to guarantee that there will never again be a universal flood:

> Then God said to Noah and to his sons with him, "Behold, I establish my covenant with you and your descendants after you, and with every living creature that is with you, the birds, the cattle, and every beast of the earth with you, as many as came out of the ark. I establish my covenant with you, that never again shall all flesh be cut off by the waters of a flood, and never again shall there be a flood to destroy the earth" (Gen. 9:8–11).

God has kept that promise. There have been many local floods since that time but never a universal one, never again a flood to destroy all flesh. By this promise God indicates that he has changed his method of judgment. It is not that there will not come a judgment of humanity again; the New Testament tells us there will be one, not by water but by fire. But God is thus saying: I will not judge in this way again, by water, which symbolizes an accumulative judgment. It is only when water backs up, builds up, and comes in vast quantities that it becomes a danger to human life. Such accumulation permits a time of fancied safety before the judgment suddenly strikes. That is the nature of a flood. But judgment will come, God says, by fire. The amazing thing about fire is that it is latent everywhere. Strike a rock and fire leaps out. Fire is everywhere. It is God's symbolic way of teaching us that the judgment he will bring is one that is already occurring in a limited degree right now. We can see *immediately* what the results of human evil are; we do not need to wait until some final catastrophe. There is no excuse, therefore, for being caught napping, even though some will.

Love Light

Finally, the eighth and last provision is to give a sign of assurance:

And God said, "This is the sign of the covenant which I make between me and you and every living creature that is with you, for all future generations: I set my bow in the cloud, and it shall be a sign of the covenant between me and the earth. When I bring clouds over the earth and the bow is seen in the clouds, I will remember my covenant which is between me and you and every living creature of all flesh; and the waters shall never again become a flood to destroy it and remember the everlasting covenant between God and every living creature of all flesh that is upon the earth." God said to Noah, "This is the sign of the covenant which I have established between me and all flesh that is upon the earth" (Gen. 9:12–17).

That is wonderful. It is the longest section of this covenant, for it is where God puts his emphasis. He repeats it again and again. He sets a rainbow against the darkness of the clouds and says that the rainbow, that sign of glory, grace, and hope is his guarantee to us that there will never come another flood like this. How peculiarly appropriate a rainbow is. As you know, it is produced by the very elements that threaten. It is set in the midst of storm and darkness as a sign of God's grace. There are some who think that perhaps the rainbow never appeared before in human history, and this is its first appearance. That may be true. Or, perhaps this is the first time it is invested with this significance. But it is a beautiful sign of glory and of grace. It is love's light, breaking through the darkness of man's evil, in an evil world.

Do you get the message? God is speaking to us. He is speaking in the dependability of nature upon which we rest, in the fear the animals have of us, in the meat that is on our table, in the violence that sweeps America from time to time, in the teeming misery of our crowded slums and ghettos. God is speaking through all these things, driving home one fact and one alone: "The imagination of man's heart is evil continually from his youth." There is nothing you can do about it yourself. You cannot change the picture alone. All your best efforts to correct this will only make it worse. God has provided a Redeemer, a Savior, and there is no escape apart from him. That is the whole message. Are you willing to face the facts of life and give up this insane struggle to make yourself what you cannot be apart from Jesus Christ? Will you receive the offer of God's love and grace to lead you to the rainbow of fulfillment, of promise, of glory—all that he wants to make of humanity? I am not talking about heaven; I am talking about life, now. God loves us. God is grieved by the distortion of humanity which he sees on every side. He wants to make us men and women living in peace, blessing, strength, glory, and grace as he intended us to live. It can only be done through the One who came to set us free from the octopus-grip of evil that resides in each individual heart. That is the message. God has ordained all of life to keep thrusting that in front of you until you see it and are willing to turn, repent, and believe the grace of God.

Open our eyes, Father, to life around us. Help us to understand ourselves. Above all, help us to see the love which is behind every activity of yours on our behalf, love that wants to set us free, love that pleads for a chance, love that seeks a thousand ways to break through our stubborn pride and to bring us to the end of ourselves, to trust in the One who is designed to be the way by which we are to live. "Man shall not live by bread alone but by every word that proceeds from the mouth of God." "He that does not eat my flesh and drink my blood has no life in him." Lord, we pray that we might learn these lessons of life; that every one who has been struggling against the will and word of God, will turn and repent and receive the gift of grace and of life in Jesus Christ. We pray in his name, Amen.

10

The Three Families of Man

PERHAPS NO PASSAGE of the Scripture is more helpful and significant to aid us in understanding society than the latter half of Genesis 9. Here we shall learn the true divisions of mankind and also of the existence of a very dangerous trait that infects society, breaking out in sexual perversions from time to time and place to place. This will help us greatly in understanding what is happening in our own time. In Genesis 9:18–19 is a brief summary of the passage.

> The sons of Noah who went forth from the ark were Shem, Ham, and Japheth. Ham was the father of Canaan. These three were the sons of Noah; and from these the whole earth was peopled.

We tend to categorize people by their skin color, their

language, or the color of their hair or eyes. These rather superficial distinctions are the basis for our division of mankind. We speak of the white race, the yellow race, the black race, and so forth. But here in this passage we learn that there is only one race, as we have seen from the beginning in the Scriptures, but there are three *families* of mankind.

In chapter 10 we will go on to trace the spread of these families which were headed by Shem, Ham, and Japheth and learn to which division of mankind each of us belongs. But here in chapter 9 we learn the distinctive contribution that each family group is intended to make to the human race. Each contribution is different, unique, and it can be demonstrated in society that this is why God has divided the race into three families. Because sociologists have lost sight of this secret, for the most part, many of their ideas and concepts about society are faulty. We need very much to return to an understanding of this passage.

These divisions have already been hinted at in the order of the names of the sons of Noah. It is remarkable how much significance in Scripture hinges upon apparently trivial distinctions—especially in the matter of order. The *way* things are listed is often very important in the Scriptures. In Genesis 9:24 we are told that Ham was the youngest son of Noah. In the normal Hebrew listing of the names of a man's sons they would be given in chronological order, beginning with the eldest. Although it is uncertain which of the three sons was the oldest, it is remarkable that every time these three are referred to together in Scripture, it is always Shem, Ham, and Japheth, with the youngest in the middle. The explanation is in the prophecy that is given a little further on in this chapter.

The Father of Canaan

Notice also in these opening verses of the passage that we are told a specific thing about Ham—that he was the father of Canaan. This is Scripture's way of turning the spotlight upon a highly significant episode in the life of Ham, an incident which has impact upon society even yet to this day. It is essential to the understanding of society that we explore and discover what is involved in this incident recorded in the next verses:

> Noah was the first tiller of the soil. He planted a vine-yard; and he drank of the wine, and became drunk, and lay uncovered in his tent. And Ham, the father of Canaan, saw the nakedness of his father, and told his two brothers outside. Then Shem and Japheth took a garment, laid it upon both their shoulders, and walked backward and covered the nakedness of their father; their faces were turned away, and they did not see their father's nakedness. When Noah awoke from his wine and knew what his youngest son had done to him, he said, "Cursed be Canaan; a slave of slaves shall he be to his brothers" (Gen. 9:20–25).

Four things in this passage are of great interest to us: the drunkenness of Noah; the strange act of Ham, Noah's son; the filial respect that is shown by Shem and Japheth; and the cursing of Canaan, Noah's grandson, the son that was actually involved in this incident, in place of Ham. Notice that this is a condensed account of this event, evident in the fact that Noah's drunkenness occurred some considerable time after they had left the ark. There was time to plant a vineyard, time to allow it to grow to fruitbearing maturity (anywhere from three to five years), time to harvest a crop, to gather it and extract the juice from the grapes, and time to allow it to ferment into wine. At last, Noah drinks of this wine, becomes drunk, and lies uncovered in his tent.

It is difficult to know what to make of the drunkenness of Noah. There have been some scholars who suggest that it means that fermentation had never occurred before on the earth, that the conditions that prevailed before the flood were quite different from today, and that probably there had never been fermentation before. Therefore, Noah would not know what was going to happen to him when he drank so much wine, and this explains his drunkenness. There may be something to this, but it is impossible to be dogmatic about it. It may have been either an act of innocence or of self-indulgence. Certainly there is no blame expressed toward Noah in this account, even though afterward drunkenness is everywhere condemned in Scripture and regarded as sin.

Noah evidently felt warm because of the effect of the alcohol, took off his clothes, and fell asleep in his tent, or, as we say of drunken persons, he "passed out" and lay exposed in the tent. Just exactly what his son did to him is also very difficult to determine. There are some Bible scholars who link this episode with the account in Leviticus 18, where, under the law, "to see the nakedness" of an individual is a euphemistic expression for a sexual act. Some scholars feel that Ham committed some homosexual act. At the very least, it is clear that Ham looked upon his father in his exposed condition with a leering glance that had sexual connotations. Whether or not there was outright homosexuality, it is clear that some form of sexual perversion is indicated either in thought or in act.

In order to understand this incident we must recall the

conditions that existed before the flood and which produced the flood. In Genesis 6 we saw that a demonic invasion of the human race occurred which was very similar to what we see in the New Testament in the days of our Lord. The result of this was a widespread outbreak of sexual perversion. Shem, Ham, and Japheth grew up in this kind of an atmosphere; Noah and his family were an island of righteousness in the midst of a sea of perversion that had possessed society before the flood. Though Ham perhaps was no pervert himself, nevertheless, it is clear from this account that he regarded this whole matter of the exposure of his father in a lurid way. He was ready to take a lewd delight in joking about this episode, even with respect to his own father. This reflects how much impact the sexually distorted society in which these boys grew up had upon Ham.

It is also noteworthy here that Shem and Japheth would have nothing to do with this; they did not respond to their brother's suggestiveness. They exemplify in action the verse in the New Testament, "Love covers a multitude of sins" (1 Pet. 4:8). Literally they covered their father and refused to look upon his shame; thus they honored their father and won the approval and blessing of God.

Noah Had a Reason

But perhaps the strangest thing in this whole account is that when Noah awoke and learned what Ham had done, he did not curse Ham, but rather settled the curse upon Canaan, the youngest of Ham's four sons. The question that leaps out as we read this account is: why does Noah curse Canaan instead of Ham? We cannot take this as mere caprice on Noah's part. There is some reason for this, and the discovery of that reason is an open door into further understanding of society. Noah knew a great deal more about human society than most people do today.

Noah evidently knew that sexual perversion is linked with parental influence, both through an inherited weakness, and environmentally. That is one of the things that psychology is telling us today. Psychologists who have made a study of homosexuality say that most homosexuals come from homes where there is a distorted parental influence. Homosexuality in men can usually be traced to a dominant mother and a weak father, and the opposite is true for homosexual women. We need to understand this in these days when this perversion is widespread and generally accepted. As we saw in Genesis 6, there is a suggestion of an outright genetic link, an inheritance factor is involved. If this is the case, as I strongly suspect it is, then Noah knew that Ham's tolerance of perversion, his delight in it, would break out in an intensified form in at least one of his children. Thus, guided by divine wisdom, he unerringly selects the one boy of Ham's four sons in whom this perversion will find outlet and expression. So the curse is pronounced upon Canaan. We must realize that the Bible understands us much better than we do ourselves. The one area in which we consistently fail to understand society is in recognizing the links between human beings, especially between parents and children— the effect of one generation upon another. It is made clear here that Noah knows that though in Ham this perversion may not manifest itself any more openly than a mere tolerance and acceptance of it, yet in his son it will be greatly intensified. Therefore, the curse rests upon Canaan.

Now all this is proved in the book of Joshua (and also in 1 Kings) where we are told that the Canaanite tribes are all descendants of Canaan. They are listed for us in Genesis 10:15, "Canaan became the father of Sidon his first-born, and Heth, and the Jebusites, the Amorites, the Girgashites, the Hivites, the Arkites, the Sinites, the Arvadites, the Zemarites, and the Hamathites." The names of these tribes appear many times throughout Old Testament history. These were the inhabitants of the land of Canaan when Israel came up out of Egypt. It was because of the moral turpitude of these people, who lived in sexually perverted ways, that God commanded the children of Israel to exterminate them when they came into the land. This bothers a great many people when they study the Old Testament; how can God order a whole people wiped out? Well, there was good reason for it. These people were a moral blight upon society, and it was necessary for them to be totally eliminated in order to preserve society from the deterioration and degradation that they represented. When Israel failed to do this, they became, as the curse of Canaan here suggests, ". . . hewers of wood and carriers of water," a servant of servants to the people of Israel, as recorded in Joshua 9:23.

Now, all this answers a very widespread distortion of this passage that has been accepted for many, many years which says that the curse of Noah fell on the Negro people. The mark of it was a black skin, and, therefore, they are destined to be servants among mankind. But the Canaanites, as far as we know, were not black people. The curse was wholly fulfilled in Joshua's day when these descendants of Canaan, morally perverted through this evil strain which had survived the flood and then broke out again in human history, were left alive by Israel. Thus, there was loosed in society an evil element which has spread throughout the entire race since, and breaks out in sexual perversions from place to place. (There is, however, a grain of truth in applying this passage to the Negro people. Powerful lies gain their power from having at least a modicum of truth about them. It is true that the colored peoples of the earth are descendants of Ham—Hamitic people. They come in varying shades; the yellow of the Chinese, the brown of the Indians, the black of the Africans, and even include some that are white-skinned.)

Now we must turn to the prophetic words uttered by Noah about his sons as to the destiny of their descendants:

He *also* said (notice how he deliberately sets this apart from what he said about Canaan),

"Blessed by the Lord my God be Shem; and let Canaan be his slave. God enlarge Japheth, and let him dwell in the tents of Shem; and let Canaan be his slave." After the flood Noah lived three hundred and fifty years. All the days of Noah were nine hundred and fifty years; and he died (Gen. 9:26–29).

Here we have the three families of mankind. The family of Ham is represented by Canaan, although not limited to his descendants. In certain of the old versions, in these two verses referring to Canaan, the account reads, "Ham, the father of Canaan," which is probably the more accurate rendering. Now this is a most important passage. We can hardly overrate its importance in understanding the world of our day.

Notice that Shem is given religious primacy among mankind. The Semitic people, the descendants of Shem, were responsible under God to meet the spiritual needs of mankind. That is their role in humanity. It is most striking that the three great religions of earth all come from the

Semitic family: Judaism, Mohammedanism, and Christianity. There is much distortion of truth in these, granted, but the sense of mission by the Semitic families of earth is very evident. This family includes the Jews, the Arabs, certain ancient peoples, as well as other modern groups.

Japheth was promised enlargement. The Japhetic people are, in general, the peoples of India and Europe, the Indo-European stock. It is largely from this family that we Americans come. It is most interesting that history has recorded their geographical enlargement. The entire western hemisphere of our globe is settled by Japhetic peoples, and the Indians (Hindus) are of the same stock. But there is much in history to suggest that the enlargement promised here to Japheth is also intellectual. Historically, all the great philosophers are Japhetic. The Greeks, who founded modern philosophy, are descendants of Japheth, as we will see in the next chapter, also the Hindus. The Greeks and the Hindus are the two truly great philosophic races of earth. You may object that Confucius, a Hamite, should be considered here, but Confucius was not a philosopher; he was a teacher of practical ethics.

A very astute Christian scholar has been a great help to me in various fields of Bible study. His name is Dr. Arthur Custance, from Brockville, Ontario, to whom I am greatly indebted for some of these concepts. He takes the phrase, ". . . let him (Japheth) dwell in the tents of Shem" as predictive of the Cross, when the spiritual guidance of humanity passed from the Jews to the Gentiles, i.e., from Shem to the Japhetic family. To Shem was given the primacy of religious teaching, but there comes a time when Japheth enters that field ("dwells in the tents of Shem"), and philosophy (which is essentially Japhetic) was married to theology. This has been the case since the dispersion of the Jews around the world.

The Great Inventors

There is much more we will say on this as we go on into chapter 10, but let me speak briefly about Ham. Ham is given the role of a servant in relation to both of these other families of earth. But notice carefully, he was not a servant in the sense of enslavement. That role was limited to the descendants of Canaan. "A slave of slaves," is the Hebrew way of emphasizing, of intensifying, a statement. Canaan was to be a slave, but the rest of the sons of Ham were to fulfill a servant relationship as the practical technicians of humanity. If you study ancient history, you will learn that all the earliest civilizations, with their discoveries and technological achievements which were in many ways the equal or superior of much that we have today, were founded and carried to a high technological proficiency by Hamitic people. This is the role in history given by God to the descendants of Ham. The Egyptians, the Babylonians, the Mayans, the Aztecs, all were Hamitic people. They were the great inventors of mankind. It may come as a shock to some, who think of Americans as the most inventive people on the earth, to know that almost every basic invention can be traced to the Hamites, rather than to the Japhethites, which we represent. All that Japhetic people do is to develop the philosophy of science and applied technology, but the actual discoveries are largely traceable to the Hamitic peoples of the earth.

Now, to bring this introduction of the subject to a conclusion, all of this is reflected most interestingly in the New Testament. We have, for instance, the so-called Synoptic Gospels (Matthew, Mark, and Luke), which are very similar to one another and quite different from the Gospel of John. Yet Matthew, Mark, and Luke are not copies of one another, but they represent different approaches; they are aimed at different types of people. The interesting thing is that when you inquire as to the identity of these people, you find that they are Shem, Ham, and Japheth, in that order. Matthew is aimed at the Semitic people. It is the Gospel for the Jews, above all others. Mark is clearly the Gospel of the servant. This is stressed by Bible teachers whenever they teach Mark; his Gospel is profoundly the presentation of the servant, the practical mind, the Hamitic mind. Luke is clearly aimed at the Greek, or the Japhetic mind.

It is also interesting that three groups are recorded in the New Testament as specifically coming to seek the Lord Jesus. They are the shepherds, the wise men, and the Greeks. Here again the order is repeated: Shem, Ham, and Japheth. The shepherds were Israelites, Semitic. Most Bible scholars feel that the Magi, the wise men from the East, were really not from the East (that was a general term) but from Arabia, and represented the Hamitic peoples. The Greeks are clearly Japhethites. So there again, always in the same order, we have Shem, Ham, and Japheth.

Also, the gospel was first preached in this order. In the book of Acts we are told that on the day of Pentecost Peter stood up and said, "Ye men of Israel," and addressed the gospel to them. Then in the next section we find Philip called to leave a revival in Samaria and go down to preach to a single individual in the desert, who is a Hamite, an Ethiopian, the treasurer of Ethiopia. Then, a little bit later on Peter is sent to the Japhethites, preaching the gospel to Cornelius, a centurion of Rome.

Furthermore, all three of these groups are represented at the crucifixion. Each branch of mankind took part in the crucifixion. The moral responsibility for it fell upon the Jews. It is they who said, "His blood be upon us and upon our children." The physical burden of bearing the cross fell upon a Hamite, Simon of Cyrene (a part of North Africa), a stranger in Jerusalem who was impressed into the task of bearing the cross for our Lord on the Via Dolorosa. Finally, as you know, executive responsibility for the crucifixion rested with the Romans, who gave the official order for the death of our Lord.

The Inner Balance

Now we shall see much more of this in chapter 10, but I think this is enough to show how accurately the Bible previews history and how it deals realistically with these matters. There are often hidden in these biblical passages amazing truths which, when we once begin to trace them, carry us into vast and exciting fields of discovery. We have looked at enough to confirm to us this fact: the race, the whole race, is but the individual written large. There are three divisions of mankind, as there are three divisions in man, in you. To each of these divisions is given the responsibility for meeting one of the basic needs of man: spiritual, physical, and intellectual. In each one of us these same three divisions are found. We have a capacity to worship; we have a capacity to reason; and we have a capacity to work with our hands. These are the things that distinguish us from the animals. This is the image of God in man. Each of them needs to be held in perfect balance. The world is in a state of confusion, uncertainty, and despair because the balance God intended has been left unfulfilled. So also, in your individual life you may be in a state of confusion, despair, frustration, weakness, or whatever, because you have neglected to fulfill the three-fold capacities of your own nature.

It is wrong to think of man as primarily spiritual. He is also intellectual and physical. It is wrong to think of him as being essentially physical, developing athletic abilities to the neglect of the others; he is also spiritual and intellectual. The interesting thing is that in the Bible the intellectual is put last. If the order of Scripture obtains for the individual as well as for the race, the order within us is also Shem, Ham, and Japheth. First the spiritual, then the physical, then the intellectual. In that order mankind finds its complete fulfillment. If we understand ourselves, we will also understand the world around us. The glory of the gospel is that it addresses itself to mankind exactly on those terms. We find ourselves being what we were intended to be when we open our lives to God through Jesus Christ, making that priority number one; then developing the physical life, taking care of physical needs, physical demands; and through these two working together, developing the intellectual to an understanding of ourselves.

Surely we can echo these words of David in the eighth Psalm:

> O lord, our Lord, how majestic is thy name in all the earth! . . . what is man that thou art mindful of him? . . . Thou hast given him dominion over the works of thy hands; thou hast put all things under his feet.

Man is to fulfill that destiny as he finds fulfillment in the Son of God.

Thank you again, our Father, for instruction from your word. The Word of God is given, we are told, to instruct us in righteousness. Now we pray that we may be open to this instruction and understand life and ourselves because of its revelation to us. Make us to realize how essential it is that we begin at the beginning. "The fear of the Lord is the beginning of wisdom." We pray, therefore, that we may bow before you, our God, our Maker, our Redeemer, our Friend, our Savior, and let our hearts respond in love and gratitude to you who desire to make us exactly what you intended us to be. We pray in Christ's name, Amen.

11
God's Funnel

WE COME NOW to Genesis 10, a very difficult chapter. I shall ask you to be patient with me as we look at it together. You may not find it quite what you feel you need, for although it is quite fascinating to study, it is exceedingly dreary to read. You may ask, "Why should we spend time with a passage like this?" In answer, I would say that it is extremely important that we understand God's movements in history. This chapter helps us realize and accept the fact that what we read in Scripture about eternal life and the things of the Spirit is realistic and true to life around us, that we are dealing with the Word of God and therefore with life as it really is. Perhaps we can see this most clearly in a chapter like this.

Chapter 10 of Genesis is a record of how mankind fanned out over all the earth, like spokes in a wheel, radiating from a center which both science and Scripture place in the Middle East. The Middle East has been called, "The cradle of civilization": or "The cradle of mankind." We could spend hours in chapter 10 tracing the development of these families of man. This is the kind of chapter that requires careful and exhaustive study, but I shall merely attempt a quick survey, pausing where Moses (the author of Genesis) also pauses to comment on certain names that appear in this section. These are important comments and we need to understand why Scripture suddenly turns the spotlight upon certain individuals. The division begins with Japheth and his descendants:

> These are the generations of the sons of Noah, Shem, Ham, and Japheth; sons were born to them after the flood. The sons of Japheth: Gomer, Magog, Madai, Javan, Tubal, Meshech, and Tiras. The sons of Gomer: Ashkenas, Riphath, and Togarmah. The sons of Javan: Elishah, Tarshish, Kittim, and Dodanim. From these the coastland peoples spread. These are the sons of Japheth in their lands, each with his own language, by their families, in their nations (Gen. 10:1–5).

This division of the chapter, centering on Japheth, is the shortest. Yet to us in many ways it is the most important because it is to this family of mankind that most of us belong. We are Japhethites, and we find this of intense interest, although the Scripture spends the least time with it.

Those who study races and peoples are known as ethnologists, and one of the tools of ethnology is to trace the persistence of names through history. Some of these place names and names of individuals persist for a long time through the course of human events and form a kind of peg upon which we can hang certain important movements in history and by which we can trace certain developments. We can do this with many of the names in this passage. Letters may be transposed, endings added, prefixes taken away or added, but there is a basic root which persists for years and even centuries of time, and these give us a way of tracing the spread of the peoples of earth.

The family of Japheth is essentially what we call the Aryans. Hitler made much of the Aryan race, claiming that the Germans were pure Aryans and the rest were mongrels. Of course, the Jews were of a completely different family; he was right about that, for the Jews are Semitic (from Shem), while the Aryans are from Japheth. But where Hitler made his mistake (and where many people today make a mistake) was to confuse differences between people with supposed superiority based on these differences. Because people are different is no sign that they are inferior or superior. This is one of the basic things we need to understand in studying the peoples of the earth.

Indian Cousins

Early in the history of the world, the Japhethites, or Aryans, split into two groups. One group settled in India and the other group in Europe. Together they form what is known as the "Indo-European" family of nations. Any ethnographer is familiar with these divisions, but they are the same basic stock. The next time you visit India you should realize that you are visiting your cousins in the same basic family. The interesting thing is that both of these divisions, the Indian and the European, trace their ancestry back to Japheth. This is not from the Bible but from history. The Greeks say that their ancestor was a man named Japetos, and you can see in that name the resemblance to Japheth. They regarded him as not only the father of their race but the father of all humanity. The Indians, on the other hand, have an account of the flood similar in many respects to the biblical account. The name of their hero is not Noah, but Satyaurata, and he had three sons. The name of the oldest was Iyapeti (you can see Japheth in that very easily), and the other two were Sharma, and C'harma (Shem and Ham). The interesting thing about the Indian account is that C'harma was cursed by his father because he laughed at him when he got drunk—a certain echo of the story we have in Genesis. You see from this how this chapter is embedded in history. The Word of God is dealing with realistic matters when it traces these divisions.

We learn here that Japheth had seven sons, but only two of them are traced for us in any detail. The first son was Gomer. From this word, Gomer, by a process of elision and transposition of letters, came the word, Gaul, or Gallic. These are the people, interestingly enough, to whom the New Testament Epistle to the Galatians is written. The Galatians were Gauls. Most of us have a Gallic or Celtic (or Keltic) ancestry, and the Gauls and Celts (or Kelts) were descendants of Gomer. They migrated to the north and settled in Spain, France, Germany and in Britain. From these Gauls come most of the early families of Western Europe and, consequently, of the Americas as well.

The oldest son of Gomer was Ashkenaz. He and his descendants first settled around the Black Sea and then moved north into a land which is called Ascenia, later known as the Islands of Scandia, which we now know as Scandinavia. You can trace a direct link between Ashkenaz and Scandinavia. Another of the sons of Gomer was Riphath. Although we do not know too much about Riphath we do know that he located in Central Europe, and some scholars feel that the word *Europe* itself comes from this name, Riphath. Another son is Togarmah. This name is easily traced. He was the ancestor of the present-day Turks and Armenians, who also migrated northward into Southern Germany. Certain scholars have felt that the word *Germany* derives from the word Togarmah. If you drop the first syllable, you have the basic root of Germany.

Two others of the sons of Japheth were Madai and Javan. These are easily recognizable in history. The Madai became the Medes, of the famous Medes and Persian Empire. Javan is unquestionably the ancestor of the Greeks. The name, Javan, is still found in Greece in the form of Ionia. The Ionic Sea, and Ionic Peninsula all derive from this word, Javan. His sons were Elishah, from which we get the Greek word, Helles (the Greeks are still called "Hellenes") and Tarshish whom most scholars associate with Spain; Kittim, which is the Island of Cyprus; and Dodanim, who settled around the Black Sea, and still finds a modern parallel in the word, the Dardanelles. These can all be traced by the geographical titles and place names they left behind.

Pioneers of Mankind

Next is the family of Ham, which is the family gifted with technical proficiency. Because of the great adaptability of these people to primitive conditions, the Hamites became the great pioneers of mankind. All the early civilizations were Hamitic: the Egyptians, the Babylonians, the Mayans, the Aztecs, the Sumerians. These were the people most able to adapt themselves to the conditions they found wherever they settled. We owe a great deal to the Hamitic nations. Later on, these lands were occupied by Japhetic nations and presently the entire Western hemisphere is peopled by Japhetic rather than Hamitic nations, though it was once the other way around.

We shall take the family of Ham in two sections, briefly commenting on certain items.

The sons of Ham: Cush, Egypt, Put, and Canaan. The sons of Cush: Seba, Havilah, Sabtah, Raamah, and Sabteca. The sons of Raamah: Sheba and Dedan. Cush became the father of Nimrod; he was the first on earth to be a mighty man. He was a mighty hunter before the Lord; therefore it is said, "Like Nimrod a mighty hunter before the Lord." The beginning of his kingdom was Babel, Erech, and Accad, all of them in the land of Shinar. From that land he went into Assyria, and built Nineveh, Rehoboth-Ir, Calah, and Resen between Nineveh and Calah; that is the great city. Egypt became the father of Ludim, Anamim, Lehabim, Naphtuhim, Pathrusim, Casluhim (whence came the Philistines), and Caphtorim (Gen. 10:6–14).

The four sons of Ham are relatively easy to trace in history. Cush is associated with the peoples of Southern Arabia and Ethiopia. Ethiopians still trace their ancestry back to Cush. Egypt (or Mizraim, in Hebrew—an ancient name for Egypt) became the father of the Egyptian Empire, settling in the Nile Valley. Put is associated with Lydia, on the west of Egypt in North Africa. Canaan centered largely in and around Palestine, though the Canaanites later became much more widespread.

The account zooms in on an individual named Nimrod, who is called a great hunter. He is a rather mysterious figure of great importance in ancient history. He is the founder of both Babylon and Nineveh, the two great cities of antiquity which became, ultimately, enemies of Israel. The prominent thing that is said about him here is that he was a mighty man, a mighty hunter before the Lord. Now, it was the work of kings in those ancient days to be hunters. This was a time when civilization was sparse and wild animals were a constant threat to the people. Kings, having nothing much else to do, organized hunting parties and acted as the protectors of their people by killing wild animals. Nimrod evidently gained a great reputation as such a hunter, but he was more than a hunter of wild animals. The Jewish Talmud helps us here, for it says that he was "a hunter of the souls of men." By the founding of Babylon and Nineveh we have a hint given of the nature of this man. We are told here that he was "the first mighty man on earth," i.e., after the flood. That phrase, "mighty man," takes us back to Genesis 6 where, in that strange story of the invasion of the "sons of God" into the human race, there resulted a race of giants called Nephilim. We are told that "these were the mighty men that were of old, the men of renown." This demonic invasion of the race, with sexual overtones, brought into being a race of giants that were morally degraded. These also appear later on in the Canaanite tribes. We have found this suggestive line of thought running through the Scriptural account up to this point. Nimrod apparently was one of these "mighty men," and therefore introduced a perverted, degraded form of religion into the world. It began at Babylon, spread to Nineveh, and can be traced in history as it subsequently spread throughout the whole of the earth. Thus, in this man Nimrod, we have the seed of idolatry and false religion coming in again after the flood.

Mother and Child Cult

If you drop the first consonant of Nimrod's name and take the others—M, R, D—you will have the basic root of the god of Babylon, whose name was Marduk, and whom most scholars identify with Nimrod. In the Babylonian religion, Nimrod (or Marduk) held a unique place. His wife was Semiramis. (In Cairo, Egypt, the Semiramis Hotel is named after this woman.) Marduk and Semiramis were the ancient god and goddess of Babylon. They had a son whom Semiramis claimed was virgin-born, and they founded the mother and child cult. This was the central character of the religion of ancient Babylon, the worship of a mother and child, supposedly virgin-born. You can see in this a clever attempt on the part of Satan to anticipate the genuine virgin birth and thus to cast disrepute upon the story when the Lord Jesus would later be born into history.

This ancient Babylonian cult of the mother and child spread to other parts of the earth. You will find it in the Egyptian religion as Isis and Osiris. In Greece it is Venus and Adonis, and in the Hindu religion it is Ushas and Vishnu. The same cult prevails in various other localities. It appears in the Old Testament in Jeremiah where the Israelites are warned against offering sacrifices to "the Queen of Heaven." This Queen of Heaven is Semiramis, the wife of Nimrod, the original mother of the Mother and Child cult. The cult has also crept into Christianity and forms the basis for the Mariolatry that has prevailed in the Roman Catholic Church, where the Mother and Child are worshiped as joint redeemers. Alexander Hislop, an authoritative writer in this field, has written a book called "The Two Babylons," which should be of great interest if you desire to pursue this further.

This idolatrous religion culminates at last in the Bible in the book of Revelation. There, a "great harlot" appears, whose name is "Mystery Babylon the Great," the originator of all the harlotries and false religions of earth. The essence of Babylonianism, as we understand from Scripture, is the attempt to gain earthly honor by means of religious authority. That is Babylonianism, and it has pervaded Christian churches, Hindu temples, Buddhist shrines, and Mohammedan mosques. Everywhere it is the element that marks falseness in religion—the attempt to gain earthly power and prestige by means of religious authority. That is what Nimrod began and what God will ultimately destroy, as we read in the book of Revelation.

The land of Shinar, mentioned here, is also the land of Shunar or Shumar from which we get the word, Sumeria, and the Sumerian civilization with which scholars are familiar. The city of Resen was founded by people who later migrated into the north of Italy and began the great Etruscan empire which again is familiar to any who study ancient history. We also have here the countries that came from Egypt and are associated with it, all of which are countries of North Africa. One further note on this section: the Philistines, which appear frequently elsewhere in the Old Testament, are linked with the Egyptians. This is significant, for Egypt in the Bible is always a picture of the world, and the Philistines are a picture of the flesh in its religious aspect, Pharisaism, if you like. These are forever typified by these two nations.

The second section of the sons of Ham centers on the descendants of Canaan:

> Canaan became the father of Sidon his first-born, and Heth, and the Jebusites, the Amorites, the Girgashites, the Hivites, the Arkites, the Sinites, the Arvadites, the

Zemarites, and the Hamathites. Afterward the families of the Canaanites spread abroad. And the territory of the Canaanites extended from Sidon, in the direction of Gerar, as far as Gaza, and in the direction of Sodom, Gomorrah, Admah, and Zeboiim, as far as Lasha. These are the sons of Ham, by their families, their languages, their lands, and their nations (Gen. 10:15–20).

We have already seen that these constituted the morally degraded Canaanite tribes which occupied the land of Palestine at the time of Abraham. We must note certain individuals in this listing, but not all. Sidon is mentioned as the first-born of Canaan. He founded the city by the same name, located near Tyre on the coast of Phoenicia. The fact that there is no mention of Tyre here indicates how early an account this is. Heth is the father of the Hittite nation. The Hittites were once regarded by archeologists as a biblical blunder; they said the Bible was absolutely wrong when it mentioned the Hittites—there were no such people. But Hittite relics have since been discovered in abundance, and scholars are now well aware of the great civilization that flourished under the Hittites. The Hebrew form of this word, Hittite, is Khettai, and from this comes the word, Cathay, which you will recognize as an ancient name for China. Certain of the Hittites migrated eastward and settled in China.

Another name in this list, the Sinites, is also linked with China. It derives from a presumed son of Canaan whose name was Sin. The Sinites migrated eastward until they came into Western China where they founded the ancient empire of China and gave their name to the land. There is a direct connection between the word, China, and the word, Sinim, the biblical name for China. I remember reading as a boy of the Sino-Japanese War, showing how the ancient name still persists. They pushed eastward and toward the north over the land bridge into Alaska. The Sinites are the people who settled the Americas in prehistoric days and became the ancestors of the Eskimos and Indians who still betray their Mongoloid ancestry.

Now the third family to be traced here is Shem.

To Shem also, the father of all the children of Eber, the elder brother of Japheth, children were born. The sons of Shem: Elam, Asshur, Arpachshad, Lud, and Aram. The sons of Aram: Uz, Hul, Gather, and Mash. Arpachshad became the father of Shelah; and Shelah became the father of Eber. To Eber were born two sons: the name of the one was Peleg, for in his days the earth was divided, and his brother's name was Joktan. Joktan became the father of Almodad, Sheleph, Hazarmaveth, Jerah, Hadoram, Uzal, Diklah, Obal, Abimael, Sheba, Ophir, Havilah, and Jobab; all these were the sons of Joktan. The territory in which they lived extended from Mesha in the direction of Sephar to the hill country of the east. These are the sons of Shem, by their families, their languages, their lands, and their nations.

These are the families of the sons of Noah, according to their genealogies, in their nations; and from these the nations spread abroad on the earth after the flood (Gen. 10:21–32).

The noteworthy thing here is that Shem was the father of the children of Eber—actually, Eber was a great-grandson of Shem—and from Eber comes the word, Hebrew. Abraham, who was really the founder of the Hebrew nation, was six generations beyond Eber. Yet Eber is of such note that Abraham is identified as an Eberite, or Hebrew. Elam, the next son of Shem, is associated with southern Mesopotamia. Archeologists have now found that the earliest inhabitants of this area were Semites, not Hamites, as they once thought. Asshur is the one who gave his name to Assyria.

The geneology closes with two sons of Eber named Peleg and Joktan. The tribes listed as from Joktan are all associated with Arabia. The boundaries of Mesha and Sephar given here are both within the Arabian peninsula. Our main interest, however, centers on Peleg and this cryptic comment made about him, ". . . in his days the earth was divided." What do you think that means? Peleg, in Hebrew, means "division," but in Greek it means "sea." We get our present English word, archipelago, from this: archi-pelagos, the first sea. The Greeks called the Aegean Sea "*The* Archipelago," the first sea, drawing the name from this man, Peleg.

There is some evidence to link this with the scientific theory of continental drift—the idea that once the continents were bound together in one great land mass, but some time in the past they separated and began to drift apart until the Americas came to their present location, Australia slid down into the south, Antarctica still further south, and the continents assumed the present distribution of land mass on the earth. Some have suggested that this may have occurred as late as the days of Peleg, immediately following the flood. Perhaps the great rift valleys of Africa and Asia had not yet formed, and in Peleg's day these drew apart so that the seas broke into this inner world and formed the Red Sea, the Mediterranean Sea, and the Dead Sea. This would be the formation of the first sea, from which we get the word, archipelago. Many geologists, of course, would raise questions about this, saying this is far too late in history for anything like that to have occurred. The account here is much too brief for us to be dogmatic about this, but it is very suggestive. It may well have been that the American continent was still in view of Europe and Asia in those days, and that as it moved westward, it gradually disappeared from the horizon. This perhaps gave rise to the many myths and stories about a lost continent called Atlantis which disappeared beneath the Atlantic.

The Funnel's Neck

Now we must come to the explanation of the title I have chosen for this chapter, "God's Funnel." A funnel, as you know, is an instrument or device for narrowing a flow of liquid or powder from a wide expanse to a narrow one. That is what God is doing here in Genesis 10. Shem is put last of the sons of Noah because God is narrowing the flow of sacred history down to the Semitic races. Shem is the neck of the funnel. God is restricting the stream of humanity that he will deal with personally and directly down to one family group, the family of Shem. In chapter 11, from verse 10 to the end of the chapter, he takes this up again and narrows it still further to one man, Abraham. From there it begins to broaden out again to take in Abraham and all his descendants, both physical and spiritual. The rest of the Bible is all about the children of Abraham, physically and spiritually. We have here, then, one of the most important links in understanding the Bible.

Now why does God do this? He has been accused of showing favoritism in picking the people of Israel for his link with humanity. But God is no respecter of persons, as we are told. He does this because it is necessary in view of the limitations of *our* minds, not of his. No one man can grasp the whole widespread, varied world of mankind. We cannot do so even today. At election time we take polls to determine what people are thinking, because we cannot grasp or assimilate in any way what the entire mass of a people are thinking. We must take polls, or samples. God is doing this with Israel. Israel becomes the sample nation, the sample people. Through the rest of the Bible, whatever is true of Israel is true of everyone; their story is our story—your story and my story. Their stubborn rebellion is the same rebellion that we display, and their spiritual blessing under God is the same kind that we can expect if we open ourselves to respond to the grace of God. One fact comes drumming through all this otherwise dry genealogy: God is seeking somehow to break through into our hearts and wills. He presses in upon us, both in the great historic sweeps and in the minor incidents that happen to each of us. But in every case it is the same truth; God is essential to us. We cannot live without God. You cannot fulfill yourself, you cannot find yourself without him. He loves you, is seeking you, wants you, and is drawing you to himself.

Our Father, we pray that we might respond to the approach you have taken such great trouble to bring about, having written it so large upon the canvas of history that we cannot miss it if we have eyes to see. Yet how little we have paid attention to this. Lord, make us serious about these matters. Make us, young and old alike, to take seriously your desires for our life and the inescapability of your presence in history. Lord, we pray that we may live with these truths, and act upon them, in Jesus' name, Amen.

12

Controlling God

IN THE PASSAGE that we come to now on the tower of Babel, we shall find the answer to one of the great mysteries of life, the mystery of a race that hungers after unity and is forever seeking to be one but is also forever splitting itself into fragments and dividing into splinters, schisms, and cliques. Why should this be so? We shall attempt an answer as we look at this passage together. We begin in the days when the race was still one undivided entity.

Now the whole earth had one language and few words. And as men migrated from the east, they found a plain in the land of Shinar and settled there. And they said to one another, "Come, let us make bricks, and burn them thoroughly." And they had brick for stone, and bitumen for mortar. Then they said, "Come, let us build ourselves a city, and a tower with its top in the heavens, and let us make a name for ourselves, lest we be scattered abroad upon the face of the whole earth" (Gen. 11:1–4).

When this account says, ". . . the earth had one language and few words," it literally is saying it had one language and one set of words. "Few words" brings to mind a certain lady in our congregation who says, "I'm a woman of few words, but I use them frequently." But what is meant here is "one speech," as the Authorized Version puts it. This is the noteworthy feature of the humanity of that day; they were still one undivided people.

The atmosphere of the previous chapter is one of movement, migration. People are thrusting out from a center, like spokes of a wheel, radiating out into the corners of the earth. This chapter opens on the same note. As men moved about they came into the plain of Shinar, an alluvial plain lying between the Tigris and the Euphrates rivers. The name Shinar indicates to us that these people were Hamites, descendants of Ham, because in chapter 10 we are told it was the Hamites who settled in the land of Shinar or Babylonia (Mesopotamia, as we know it today). It was a branch of the Hamitic family that migrated into the Tigris-Euphrates river valleys and found a level plain there upon which they settled.

Immediately the inventiveness of the Hamitic people becomes evident in the way they adapted to the environment in which they lived. They did not find rocks and stones to build with, such as they had in the land where they had previously lived, so they made bricks out of dirt and clay. Later they discovered the process of burning them, first in the sun and then in a furnace, until they became hard and impermeable—brick as we know it today. All this is given to us in one sentence in the Bible, but we know from history that it occupied a period of time. Man did not discover all this at once, but learned how to make bricks and later how to burn them. They also lacked lime for cement, so they could not make mortar as we know it. But some inventive Yankee among them discovered a tar pit which was filled with natural asphalt, and they used this natural bitumen, this asphalt, for mortar. They then had a substitute for stones and cement.

A City and a Tower

Now their success in doing these things fired their ambition. This almost always happens. When they discovered that they could invent their own materials for building, they were fired with desire to put these to work. They began to talk excitedly about building two things— a city and a tower. These two things are very revealing. Back in the story of Cain and Abel, Cain went out and built a city, illustrating the hunger of humanity to huddle together for companionship. They were not really ready to do it (as men still, obviously, are not ready to live together successfully in cities), but God's final intention is to build a city for man. Remember that Abraham looked for "a city which has foundations, whose builder and maker is God." But man was not yet ready for that. Now, here they are, again eager to build a city to satisfy the desires of body and soul. Nothing does this better than a city. Cities are centers of commercial and business life where all the needs of the body can best be met. Also, cities are centers of pleasure and culture, where all the hungers of the soul can be satisfied—hunger for beauty, art, music, all the ingredients of culture.

The tower, on the other hand, reflects the need to

satisfy the spirit of man. In these two things we can gain a fundamental understanding of the nature of man as body, soul, and spirit. All are to be satisfied in these two elementary items, the city and the tower. A number of years ago, digging in the plains of Shinar, archeologists discovered the remains of certain great towers that these early Babylonians had built. Some archeologists have felt that they may even have found the foundation of this original tower of Babel. That is very hard to determine. But they did find that the Babylonians built great towers called ziggurats, which were built in a circular fashion with an ascending spiral staircase terminating in a shrine at the top, around which were written the signs of the zodiac. Obviously, the tower was a religious building, intending to expose man to the mystery of the heavens and the greatness of God. That, perhaps, is what is meant here by the statement that they intended to build a tower with its top in the heavens. They were impressed by its greatness architecturally; that is, it was a colossal thing for the men of that day to build, and they may have thus thought of it as reaching into heaven. But they also unquestionably were thinking of it as a means of communication with God, of maintaining contact with him. God is not to be left out, you see, in the city of man. He is there, represented by this tower.

The heart of the matter, however, is made clear in these words, "Let us make a name for ourselves, lest we be scattered abroad upon the face of the whole earth." Already a haunting fear had set in. They were conscious already of a disruptive influence in their midst, of a centrifugal force that was pushing them apart so they could not live too closely together. They feared this force would ultimately scatter them abroad and leave them unknown, unhonored, and unsung, living in isolated communities where they would be exposed to great danger. This fear caused them to build a tower and a city. The ultimate motive is expressed in these words, "Let us make a name for ourselves."

A Name for Man

From that day on, this has been the motto of humanity; "Let us make a name for ourselves." I am always amused to see how many public edifices have a plaque somewhere on which the names of all the public officials who were in power when it was built are inscribed: the mayor, the head of public works, etc. "Let us make a name for ourselves" is a fundamental urge of a fallen race. It reveals one of the basic philosophies of humanism: "Glory to man in the highest, for man is the master of all things."

The fact that this was a religious tower, and yet built to make a name for man, reveals the master motive behind religion. It is a means by which man attempts to share the glory of God. We must understand this, otherwise we will never understand the power of religion as it has pervaded the earth and permeated our culture ever since. It is a way by which man seeks to share what is rightfully God's alone. This tower was a grandiose structure, and undoubtedly it was intended to be a means by which man would glorify God. Unquestionably, there was a plaque somewhere attached to it that carried the pious words, "Erected in the year —, to the greater glory of God." But it was not really for the glory of God; it was a way of controlling God, a way of channeling God by using him for man's glory. That is what man's religion has always sought to do. It is a way of making God available to us.

Man does not really want to eliminate God. It is only sporadically, and then only for a relatively brief time, that men cry out for the elimination of God. Atheism is too barren, too pessimistic, and too morally bankrupt to live with very long. The communists are finding this out. No, we need dear old God, but let's keep him under control. Do not let him get out of his place. "Don't call us, God, we'll call you." This is the fundamental philosophy of society. It is the tower of Babel all over again.

Now in the next section we get the reaction of God to all this. It is a section of exquisite irony.

> And the Lord came down to see the city and the tower, which the sons of men had built. And the Lord said, "Behold, they are one people, and they have all one language; and this is only the beginning of what they will do; and nothing that they propose to do will now be impossible for them (Gen. 11:5–6).

In certain circles the idea of a God who comes down to visit earth is regarded as an expression of a primitive concept of God. According to this concept, God lives up in heaven somewhere, but is cut off from direct communication from earth and is dependent upon certain messenger boys who travel back and forth to keep him informed. Somehow a message reaches God about man's tower, and he decides to come down and investigate. But the language of this account does not reflect such a primitive concept of God. Remember what has already been said about God in the book of Genesis. Already God has been presented as the Maker of heaven and earth, the One concerned about the minutest details of creation— the God who knows everything, sees everything, and is all-powerful.

No, this is not a primitive concept of God at all. Rather, it is an ironic expression—a humorous expression, if you please, designed to indicate to us in a very clever way the ridiculousness of this whole situation. Here is this tower that men erect, thinking that it will take God's breath away, that it will threaten him. Men think: here we are, we wild Promethean creatures; we've dared to invade the heavens! You had better watch out, God! But up in the real heavens this tower is so little that God can't even see it. It is so tiny that even the strongest telescope in heaven does not reveal it. So God says, "I'll come down and investigate." It is language designed to set in contrast the ridiculous suppositions of men with the greatness of God. He "came down" to investigate this tiny tower that men had erected.

Then, in all seriousness, we are given the divine analysis of the situation. There are three things that God took note of. First, man's unity: "And the Lord said, 'Behold, they are one people, and they have all one language.'" Second, he noted their creativity: "This is only the beginning," he said, "of what they will do." This creativity is part of the image of God which he conferred upon man—this inventiveness, this ability to think and reason, to deal in concepts and put them together and to come out with very practical applications. The nature of it is suggested here. Notice that God does not suggest that man does everything at once. Rather he builds gradually. One man discovers an idea, another man improves it, and a third man links it with another idea. So gradually inventive solutions to the technical problems of life take form. God took note of those facts: man is an inventive creature, and he is a united creature.

As a result of these two factors at work in society, God comes to a startling conclusion: "Nothing that they propose to do will now be impossible to them." That sounds rather up-to-date, does it not? That is exactly what man has thought about himself and what he is saying in a thousand ways today. He loudly announces continually, "There's nothing we can't solve, nothing we can't do." The startling thing from the Scriptures is that there is truth in that. God himself acknowledges it! He says it is true; if man puts his genius to any given, specific task, then his native creativeness and his persistent spirit will solve that problem eventually. Nothing will be prevented him.

Now look at God's action:

> "Come, let us go down, and there confuse their language, that they may not understand one another's speech." So the Lord scattered them abroad from there over the face of all the earth, and they left off building the city. Therefore its name was called Babel, because there the Lord confused the language of all the earth; and from there the Lord scattered them abroad over the face of all the earth (Gen. 11:7–9).

That is startling, is it not? Here these people had built a tower and a city in order that they not be scattered abroad over the face of the earth. But the net result is that *because* they built the tower and the city they were scattered abroad throughout the face of all the earth! They ended up doing the very thing that they feared.

An Optional God

Now why does God do this? What is behind his actions here? Is he jealous of man? Is God threatened after all by this tower of mud and slime that these men have built? Does it mean that he is afraid that men will master all things and that he cannot any longer control them so that the very foundations of the universe will be threatened? No, that is the way man wants to read this. We are always telling ourselves that we can do anything we want if we want it badly enough. Therefore, we don't need God; God is optional in human life. We are ready to dismiss him, or at least to remove him to a quiet corner of the house where he won't bother anybody except when we need him occasionally to run some special errands.

It is true, as we have already seen, that God admits that man can do things if he puts his mind to them. He can *do* anything, but what about being? That is the question. You see, there is a fatal flaw in man's thinking. What does he actually purpose or propose to do? The final answer is: to glorify himself, to be the center of things, to be the master of the universe—in other words, to be God. God knows that man is incapable of *this;* he is a creature. He is a dependent being; he always was and always will be. The very forces that he thinks he can manipulate to accomplish his aims are forces that are part of his own life, which he did not make and upon which he continually depends. Therefore, he is constitutionally incapable of being the God he attempts to be.

It is always the old, old story of the Sorcerer's Apprentice. Remember the boy who hired himself out to a Sorcerer to be his servant and to carry his water for him? Like all boys, tiring of the work, he looked around to find some easier way of getting the job done. One day when the master was away he prowled around among the Sorcerer's magical paraphernalia and found certain books with magic incantations in them. He learned a few of these and tried them out on the broom. To his amazement he found that he could command the broom to carry buckets of water. He sat back, opened a magazine, and read while the broom carried in the water, bucket after bucket. But after a bit, he detected a little moisture on the floor. To his consternation he realized that the tubs and basins were all full, and the broom was still carrying in the water. He decided he had better do something about it. He arose and uttered the magic incantation, but the broom kept on carrying in the water and dumping it on the floor. As it began to rise around his ankles, the boy panicked. He didn't know what to do. He cried out every magic word he knew, but nothing worked, and the broom kept on carrying in the buckets and dumping them on the floor. Soon the water rose around his neck, and he began to cry out in anguish, realizing that he hadn't learned enough. He was saved at the last moment by the return of the master who, in a few words, cleared up the whole situation.

For Man's Sake

That is a parable of the tower of Babel. Man in his inventiveness thinks he can master the earth. But the very solutions he works out become the bigger problems with which he can no longer cope. The whole vast scheme of things eludes him; he is not able to put them all together. Thus, for man's sake (this is the heart of it), *for man's sake*—not because God is afraid of man—but for man's sake, to protect him from himself, God says in effect, "Let us go down and confuse their language. Let us stop man, in his mad folly, from destroying himself; he is not God enough to handle the problems he has created." So God came down, and, suddenly, as the workers gathered for work one morning, they found they could not communicate with each other any more. What a scene this must have been. The foreman would give orders, but the men would shake their heads—they didn't understand. The foreman would yell, but they wouldn't get it. They would try to explain, but he couldn't understand them. You can imagine what fist-shaking, table-pounding, and yelling went on here. It was utter confusion.

The Bible plays upon the name of Babel and links it with the Hebrew word for confusion, *balal*. It says this was a veritable Babel of confusion. It is interesting that the name, Babel, means "the gate of God"; that was man's name for the tower. But ultimately "the gate of God," in man's eyes, became "confusion" in the eyes of God. Since that day, men have been divided by this confusion of tongues. It is striking that the confusion of tongues is most evident, even today, in the Hamitic families of earth. Linguists know that most of the languages of earth can be gathered into family groups, (e.g., the Indo-European family of languages), and in the Japhetic line and the Semitic line they are quite closely allied. It is not difficult to group those various tongues. But in the Hamitic languages all is utter confusion. Tribes of people, growing up close by one another, have completely different languages. It still persists into this day, and it still divides mankind.

We think we have solved this confusion by translating one language into another, but any linguist knows that language is much deeper than words; it is a basic, fundamental element, reflecting the thought, life, and cultural pattern of a people. Merely to know the words of a man's language by no means guarantees that you can communicate with the man. This confusion of language represents a loss of basic understanding between peoples, the loss of the ability to communicate at the deepest levels of thought. I was struck by what a world traveler recently said,

On my trip to Asia the word, Coca Cola, was the one word I understood in every language. It sprang out familiarly from signs written in the most alien characters.

What is wrong with a world in which this is the only word that has survived the Babylonian confusion of tongues? We can still talk to one another about Coca Cola, but not about freedom, not about God, not about what a neighbor is.

Is that not striking? The impressive thing to me is that man is still haunted today by the lack of unity. He feels the need for it. He feels that if we can only get together, if we can just cooperate, we can do anything with our technological abilities. Is that not the dream that hangs over humanity? If we can merge—this is the day of the merger, corporations are merging, nations are merging, companies are merging, churches are merging—if we can just become one great community again, then, with our technological excellence we can master the earth. The dream still endures, but God still scatters. God yet continues the confusion of tongues. This may be hard for the Wycliffe translator who is seeking to put Scripture into the various languages of the earth, but, nevertheless, it is the kindness of God that confuses the speech of men. It is God's way of preventing the ultimate catastrophe. When man at last gets together again and, under the illusion of technical ability, thinks he can master all the great and intricate mechanisms of life, we will have achieved the ultimate disaster. This is why God continues to humble men everywhere, to scatter, to humiliate, to bring low the proud. Jesus said in the opening words of the Sermon on the Mount, "Blessed are the poor in spirit [the man who has nothing, the man who has lost everything upon which he can depend, outside and inside himself] for his is the kingdom of heaven." When you no longer depend on anything in you, then God is ready to give you everything he possesses. That is the basic message of the Christian faith.

O the depth of the riches and wisdom and knowledge of God! How unsearchable are his judgments and how inscrutable his ways! (Rom. 11:33).

Who has been your counselor, Lord? What man has ever instructed you? How we need to quietly listen and remember that the "fear of the Lord is the beginning of wisdom," that without your mind we will only make a continual mess of things, both individually and as a race. Teach us this, Lord, above all else. We ask in Jesus' name, Amen.

DISCOVERY BIBLE STUDY BOOKS
OLD TESTAMENT STUDIES

Expository Studies in Genesis 2 and 3
(Understanding Man)
Ray C. Stedman

Explore the greatest mystery ever written, the story of man himself from the opening pages of Genesis. In probing the hidden secrets of sinfulness, the nature of temptation and God's revelation of redemptive grace, Ray Stedman clearly presents how unwilling God is that any should perish.

Expository Studies in Genesis 4-11
(The Beginnings)
Ray C. Stedman

"How to live in community" is the theme Ray Stedman treats in this exposition of Genesis chapters 4-11. In this presentation, we see the foundation underlying all human society for all time, including the one in which we live today.

Expository Studies in Esther
(The Queen and I)
Ray C. Stedman

A timely study of the timeless Book of Esther brings new light to bear upon the world-wide phenomenon of individuals searching for their true identity.

Expository Studies in Jeremiah
(Death of a Nation)
Ray C. Stedman

America today faces many parallels with Judah's experience of the beginning of the end. It was Jeremiah's sad duty to announce what would come to pass. These studies in Jeremiah trace the process of decline in a sobering manner. Jeremiah preached that judgment ultimately will come to those who reject God, and repentance is the only way out. Yet, declared the prophet, God can plant the seeds of new life and hope in a dying society.

The New Covenant in the Old Testament
David H. Roper

Through quotations and insightful personal observations, David Roper shows the essence of the Old Testament, revealing it to be both LAW (the revelation of God's will and character) and GRACE (God in 2 spheres: forgiveness and the offer of His infinite sources). Here is outlined new hope for today's Christian.

NEW TESTAMENT STUDIES

Expository Studies in Matthew 13
(Behind History)
Ray C. Stedman

The seven parables of Matthew 13 reveal the master clue to the mysteries of history. This thorough exposition offers scriptural explanations of history by tracing not events but principles which affect all human life during the present age.

Expository Studies in Mark 1-8
(The Servant Who Rules)
Ray C. Stedman

This book, covering Mark 1:1-8:26, is the first of an enlightening two-volume expositional study of the Gospel of Mark in which Ray C. Stedman explores in depth the life and ministry of Jesus Christ as a model for today's Christian servants.

Expository Studies in Mark 8-16
(The Ruler Who Serves)
Ray C. Stedman

"Discipleship ends in life, not in death. It ends in fulfillment and satisfaction. But the only way that we can find it is by means of a cross." This is what Jesus' disciples had to learn, and what the modern Christian can learn through this careful study of the second half of Mark. *The Ruler Who Serves* picks up the Gospel narrative in the eighth chapter of Mark where its companion volume, *The Servant Who Rules,* left off.

Jesus Teaches On Prayer
(Luke)
Ray C. Stedman

"We must be praying or fainting—there is no other alternative," Ray Stedman insists. Then in easy-to-understand terms he helps us explore why we should pray at all, and the true nature of the life of prayer as our Lord lived it.

Secrets of the Spirit
(John 13-17)
Ray C. Stedman

Here's a contemporary interpretation of one of the most meaningful passages of Scripture — the Upper Room Discourse in John 13-17 — a "handbook" for modern-day disciples seeking a deeper understanding of God's plan for their lives. This book offers a key to the very purpose of Jesus' life here on earth and the principles he lived by, as well as a penetrating profile of the Holy Spirit who enables us to draw spiritual strength from within. *Secrets of the Spirit* unlocks life-changing principles and illustrates how we can apply them to the problems and challenges of everyday living.

Authentic Christianity
(II Corinthians)
Ray C. Stedman

From II Corinthians you will discover the marks of real Christianity and the enemies *within* and *without*—and how to deal with them. A fresh and radical look at the New Covenant concept—that Jesus dies *for* us in order that he may live *in* us.

Expository Studies in Romans 1-8
(From Guilt to Glory, Vol. I)
Ray C. Stedman

With incisive expositional skill Ray Stedman deals with the first eight chapters of Romans in *From Guilt To Glory, Volume I*. He helps us see the flow of Paul's great message, by guiding us through the inner logic of Romans. The central focus is the death and resurrection of Christ, and the victory over sin and death on our behalf.

Expository Studies in Romans 9-16
(From Guilt to Glory, Vol. II)
Ray C. Stedman

This book continues the spiritual adventures of Romans, chapters 9-16. In this volume Ray Stedman illustrates and contemporizes the doctrinal truths which were introduced in Volume I.

Expository Studies in Ephesians 1-3
(Riches in Christ)
Ray C. Stedman

The Epistle to the Ephesians is the perfect source for newfound hope and joy when we are discouraged. Ray Stedman explains this teaching in easy-to-understand terms and applies them to modern life through real situations and fresh illustrations.

Body Life
(Ephesians 4)
Ray C. Stedman

The teaching concerning the church that is found in Ephesians 4 forms the core of this landmark book. The role of leaders is not to get things done or even to supervise the church. It is "to equip the saints for the work of ministry."

Expository Studies in Ephesians 6
(Spiritual Warfare)
Ray C. Stedman

A guidebook to a life of victory. Here is help in the day-to-day battle against an enemy who uses worry, resentment, fear, hostility and disappointment to destroy our sense of well-being and usefulness. This exposition of Ephesians 6 opens more of the hidden resources of Christ.

The Law That Sets You Free
(James)
David H. Roper

The Law That Sets You Free is an in-depth, verse-by-verse study of the Book of James as it addresses itself to the plight of our human condition. Suffering, oppression, affliction and many other common trials are viewed in the stark light of reality. The words of James enable us to "hang in," to endure, even to overcome.

OTHER DISCOVERY BIBLE STUDY BOOKS

Basics of Bible Interpretation
Bob W. Smith

A handbook on making the Bible a book you can call your own. Bob Smith leads you through a process in four phases: Back to Basics, Figurative Language, Biblical Languages, and Structural Analysis. He covers a host of subject areas, including: The Goal of Bible Study; Interpretive Principles; The Interpretive Process; Bible Study Approaches; Figures of Speech; The Language of Analogy (especially Parables); The Greeks Had a Word for It; Helps on Hebrew. A book for everyone who wants to understand what God has said to man in His Word.

Family Life: God's View of Relationships
Ray C. Stedman with David H. Roper, Jack Crabtree, Jean McAllister, John Fischer, Del Fuller

Six writers expound the Scriptures to discover God's view of relationships: in the home, in marriage, between parents and children, and with the single person. Covering both Testaments, the authors search out God's will regarding friendship, love, communication, sexuality, authority, submission, discipline, loneliness and other areas of concern for members of God's family.

When All Else Fails . . . Read the Directions
Bob W. Smith

The biblical blueprint for a vitally alive church has been tested by practical experience. The Scriptural foundation for church government shows how the body of Christ is designed to function and gives us the motivation we need for committed service.

Dying To Live
Bob W. Smith

Should counseling be left to professionals? Bob Smith says, "NO!". Any member can become a member of God's compassion corps. This introduction to "counseling that counts" is written especially for laymen. It explores the biblical foundation for practical counseling, the spiritual nature of our personal problems, and the therapy of redemption.

Love Story . . . The Real Thing
Bob W. Smith

This helpful, honest look at God's plan for love and marriage cuts through the confusion of the sexual revolution and points the way to real love, joy and fulfillment. Here's a guidebook that helps us recapture the valued ideal of God's intention for marriage.